# The Names of God

# The Names of God

## JIM HARWELL

Bridge Books

Atlanta · Chicago · Nashville

Bridge Books
4487 Post Place
Nashville, Tenn. 37205

*The Names of God.* Copyright © 2017 by Jim Harwell

All rights reserved, including the right to reproduce this book or portions thereof in any form whatsoever. For information, address:
Bridge Books Subsidiary Rights Department
4487 Post Place
Nashville, Tenn. 37205

For information about Bridge Books products, books, packages, and special discounts for bulk purchases, please contact Bridge Books info@bridgebooks.org.

Scripture references are taken from the New King James Version. © Thomas Nelson, Inc. 1992.

Cover designed by Doug McFerrin

Manufactured in the United States of America

10 9 8 7 6 5 4 3 2 1

Library of Congress

ISBN-13: 978-0-9986819-1-7

# Contents

|   | Introduction | 11 |
|---|---|---|
| 1 | Twelve Names of God | 15 |
| 2 | Fifty Names of God | 18 |
| 3 | 900+ Names of God | 26 |
| 4 | 500+ Names, Titles, Descriptions & Truths of Jesus Christ | 98 |
| 5 | The Name Jesus Christ | 118 |
|   | The Names of Jesus Christ | |
|   | Bibliography | 124 |

# Introduction

God Almighty reveals Himself to mankind in many, many ways.

In fact, He reveals Himself in so many ways, people who do not find Him and know Him are without excuse (see Romans 1:20).

One of the primary ways the one true God reveals Himself is through His names.

When God visited Moses (the burning bush passage, Exodus 3), God actually told Moses His name:

*13 Then Moses said to God, "Indeed, when I come to the children of Israel and say to them, 'The God of your fathers has sent me to you,' and they say to me, 'What is His name?' what shall I say to them?"*
*14 And God said to Moses, "I AM WHO I AM." And He said, "Thus you shall say to the children of Israel, 'I AM has sent me to you.'"*
*15 Moreover God said to Moses, "Thus you shall say to the children of Israel: 'The Lord God of your fathers, the God of Abraham, the*

*God of Isaac, and the God of Jacob, has sent me to you. This is My name forever, and this is My memorial to all generations' (Exodus 3:13-15)*

We realize the fulfillment of God's name "I AM" in Jesus Christ.

Jesus Christ said: "'Before Abraham was, I AM'" (John 8:58).

God came to earth as a man and justified Himself to the world. Jesus Christ is Lord and God, one with the Father yet separate. Amen! Glory to God!

The glorious names of God lead us to Jehovah God, the Lord God Almighty, the Creator and Sustainer of the universe. He is the great and awesome God Almighty, the only true God. He is the great I AM, the three-in-one God: the Father, the Son, and the Holy Spirit. Amen.

ONE

# Twelve Names of God

Elohim – The Creator, the Mighty One – Genesis 1:1

Jehovah Elohim – Father – Genesis 2:4

El Shaddai – Nourisher, Provider – Genesis 17:1

Adonai – Lord – Genesis 15:1-2

Jehovah Jireh – Provider – Genesis 22:14

Jehovah Rapha – Healer – Exodus 15:26

Jehovah Nissi – Victory – Exodus 17:15

Jehovah Mikkadesh – Holiness – Leviticus 20:7-8

Jehovah Shalom – Peace – Judges 6:24

Jehovah Rohi – Shepherd – Psalm 23:1

Jehovah Tsidkenu – Righteousness – Jeremiah 23:6

Jehovah Shamah – the Lord is there – Ezekiel 48:3

| Twelve Names of God | | |
|---|---|---|
| Elohim | Creator | Gen. 1:1 |
| Jehovah | Father | Gen. 2:4 |
| El Shaddai | Nourisher | Gen. 17:1 |
| Adonai | Lord | Gen. 15:1-2 |
| Jehovah Jireh | Provider | Gen 22:14 |
| Jehovah Rapha | Healer | Ex. 15:26 |
| Jehovah Nissi | Victory | Ex. 17:15 |
| Jehovah Mikkadesh | Holiness | Lev. 20:7-8 |
| Jehovah Shalom | Peace | Judges 6:24 |
| Jehovah Rohi | Shepherd | Ps. 23:1 |
| Jehovah Tsidkenu | Righteousness | Jer. 23:6 |
| Jehovah Shamah | Lord is | Ex. 48:3 |

## TWO

# 50 Names of God

1. Almighty One – "…who is and who was and who is to come, the Almighty." Rev. 1:8

2. Alpha and Omega – "I am the Alpha and the Omega, the First and the Last, the Beginning and the End." Rev. 22:13

3. Advocate – "My dear children, I write this to you so that you will not sin. But if anybody does sin, we have an advocate with the Father--Jesus Christ, the Righteous One." 1 John 2:1

4. Author and Perfecter of Our Faith – "Fixing our eyes on Jesus, the author and perfecter of faith, who for the joy set before Him en-

dured the cross, despising the shame, and has sat down at the right hand of the throne of God." Heb. 12:2

5. Authority – "Jesus said, 'All authority in heaven and on earth has been given to me." Matt. 28:18

6. Bread of Life – "Then Jesus declared, 'I am the bread of life. Whoever comes to me will never go hungry, and whoever believes in me will never be thirsty.'" John 6:35

7. Beloved Son of God – "And behold, a voice from heaven said, "This is my beloved Son, with whom I am well pleased." Matt. 3:17

8. Bridegroom – "And Jesus said to them, "Can the wedding guests mourn as long as the bridegroom is with them? The days will come when the bridegroom is taken away from them, and then they will fast." Matt. 9:15

9. Chief Cornerstone – "The stone which the builders rejected has become the chief corner stone." Ps. 118:22

10. Deliverer – "And to wait for his Son from heaven, whom he raised from the dead, Jesus who delivers us from the wrath to come." 1 Thess.1:10

11. Faithful and True – "I saw heaven standing open and there before me was a white horse, whose rider is called Faithful and True. With justice he judges and wages war." Rev.19:11

12. Good Shepherd - "I am the good shepherd. The good shepherd lays down his life for the sheep." John 10:11

13. Great High Priest – "Therefore, since we have a great high priest who has passed through the heavens, Jesus the Son of God, let us hold fast our confession." Heb. 4:14

14. Head of the Church – "And he put all things under his feet and gave him as head over all things to the church." Eph. 1:22

15. Holy Servant – "…and grant that Your bond-servants may speak Your word with all confidence, while You extend Your hand to heal, and signs and wonders take place through the name of Your holy servant Jesus." Acts 4:29-30

16. I Am – "Jesus said to them, "Truly, truly, I say to you, before Abraham was, I am." John 8:58

17. Immanuel – "…She will give birth to a son and will call him Immanuel, which means 'God with us.'" Is. 7:14

18. Indescribable Gift – "Thanks be to God for His indescribable gift." 2 Cor. 9:15

19. Judge – "…he is the one whom God appointed as judge of the living and the dead." Acts 10:42

20. King of Kings – "These will wage war against the Lamb, and the Lamb will overcome them, because He is Lord of lords and King of kings, and those who are with Him are the called and chosen and faithful." Rev. 17:14

21. Lamb of God – "The next day John saw Jesus coming toward him and said, "Look, the Lamb of God, who takes away the sin of the world!" John 1:29

22. Light of the World – "I am the light of the world. Whoever follows me will never walk in darkness, but will have the light of life." John 8:12

23. Lion of the Tribe of Judah – "Weep no more; behold, the Lion of the tribe of Judah, the Root of David, has conquered, so that he can open the scroll and its seven seals." Rev. 5:5

24. Lord of All – "For this reason also, God highly exalted Him, and bestowed on Him the name which is above every name, so that at the name of Jesus every knee will bow, of those

who are in heaven and on earth and under the earth, and that every tongue will confess that Jesus Christ is Lord, to the glory of God the Father." Phil. 2:9-11

25. Mediator – "For there is one God, and one mediator between God and men, the man Christ Jesus." 1 Tim. 2:5

26. Messiah – "We have found the Messiah" (that is, the Christ)." John 1:41

27. Mighty One – "Then you will know that I, the Lord, am your Savior, your Redeemer, the Mighty One of Jacob." Is. 60:16

28. One Who Sets Free – "So if the Son sets you free, you will be free indeed." John 8:36

29. Our Hope – "…Christ Jesus our hope." 1 Tim. 1:1

30. Peace – "For he himself is our peace, who has made the two groups one and has destroyed the barrier, the dividing wall of hostility," Eph. 2:14

31. Prophet – "And Jesus said to them, "A prophet is not without honor, except in his hometown and among his relatives and in his own household." Mark 6:4

32. Redeemer – "And as for me, I know that my Redeemer lives, and at the last He will take His stand on the earth." Job 19:25

33. Risen Lord – "…that Christ died for our sins according to the Scriptures, that he was buried, that he was raised on the third day according to the Scriptures." 1 Cor. 15:3-4

34. Rock – "For they drank from the spiritual Rock that followed them, and the Rock was Christ." 1 Cor. 10:4

35. Sacrifice for Our Sins – "This is love: not that we loved God, but that he loved us and sent his Son as an atoning sacrifice for our sins." 1 John 4:10

36. Savior – "For unto you is born this day in the city of David a Savior, who is Christ the Lord." Luke 2:11

37. Son of Man – "For the Son of Man came to seek and to save the lost." Luke 19:10

38. Son of the Most High – "He will be great and will be called the Son of the Most High. The Lord God will give him the throne of his father David." Luke 1:32

39. Supreme Creator Over All – "By Him all things were created, both in the heavens and on

earth, visible and invisible, whether thrones or dominions or rulers or authorities-- all things have been created through Him and for Him. He is before all things, and in Him all things hold together...." 1 Cor. 1:16-17

40. Resurrection and the Life – "Jesus said to her, "I am the resurrection and the life. The one who believes in me will live, even though they die." John 11:25

41. The Door – "I am the door. If anyone enters by me, he will be saved and will go in and out and find pasture." John 10:9

42. The Way – "Jesus answered, "I am the way and the truth and the life. No one comes to the Father except through me." John 14:6

43. The Word – "In the beginning was the Word, and the Word was with God, and the Word was God." John 1:1

44. True Vine - "I am the true vine, and My Father is the vinedresser." John 15:1

45. Truth – "And you will know the truth, and the truth will set you free." John 8:32

46. Victorious One – "To the one who is victorious, I will give the right to sit with me on my throne, just as I was victorious and sat down

with my Father on his throne." Rev. 3:21

47. Wonderful Counselor – Is. 9:6

48. Mighty God – Is. 9:6

49. Everlasting Father – Is. 9:6

50. Prince of Peace – "For to us a child is born, to us a son is given, and the government will be on his shoulders. And he will be called Wonderful Counselor, Mighty God, Everlasting Father, Prince of Peace." Is. 9:6

# THREE

# 949 Names and Titles of God

Christian Answers is a worldwide evangelism, education and discipleship ministry of Films for Christ, based in Washington State, USA.

1. Greek transliteration: Abba
Meaning: Father
Aramaic transliteration: Abbā—meaning: Daddy
Mark 14:36; Romans 8:15; Galatians 4:6
2. Hebrew transliteration: Abir or Abhir
Meaning: the Mighty One
3. Adam
The Last Adam or The Second Adam
1 Corinthians 15:45; Romans 5:12-21
Greek: ὁ ἔσχατος Ἀδάμ

Greek transliteration: Eschatos Adam
4. Hebrew transliteration: Adonai
Greek: Κύριος
Greek transliteration: Kyrios
5. Hebrew transliteration: Adonai Elohei-Tzva'ot
Amos 4:13 CJB, TLV
KJV: The Lord, The God of hosts
NKJV, NASB, WYC: The Lord God of hosts
NIV: The Lord God Almighty
NOG: Yahweh Elohe Tsebaoth
6. Advocate or Advocate with the Father
refers to Jesus Christ who is an advocate for his followers to the Father
1 John 2:1
7. Hebrew transliteration: `Akal `Esh
Meaning: "Consuming Fire"
Deuteronomy 4:24
8. Greek: Akrogoniaios akrogoniaios lithos
Meaning: "Chief Cornerstone"
Ephesians 2:20; 1 Peter 2:6
9. Arabic transliteration: al-ilāh or al-lāh or Allah/Allāh
Means: "the-God" and has long been used by Jews, Christians and Arabic peoples, far before the existence of Islam
Aramaic transliteration: Elah and ⊛Ĕlāhā (emphatic)
Meaning: "God"
10. The Almighty
2 Corinthians 6:18; Rev. 1:8; 19:6
11. Almighty God

Genesis 17:1; Ezek. 10:5; Rev 19:15
12. Alpha and Omega
Meaning: "The First and the Last," "The Beginning and The End"
Rev. 1:8, 11, 21:16, 22:13
13. All Sufficient
2 Corinthians 9:8
14. The Amen
refers to Jesus Christ
Revelation 3:14
15. Ancient of days
Daniel 7:9, 13-14, 22
Hebrew transliteration: `attiyq yowm
Aramaic: Atik Yomin
Greek: Palaios Hemeron
Latin: Antiquus Dierum
16. The Anointed One
refers to Jesus Christ
Acts 4:26
17. Chief Apostle
refers to Jesus Christ
18. Apostle and High Priest
refers to Jesus Christ
Hebrews 3:1
19. Atoning Sacrifice for our sins (or Propitiation for our sins)
refers to Jesus Christ
Romans 3:25; 1 John 4:10; 2:2
20. Aramaic transliteration: Attiq Yomin
Meaning: "Ancient of days"
Daniel 7:9, 13, 22
21. Author and Finisher of our faith

refers to Jesus Christ
Hebrews 12:1-2
22. Author of Eternal Salvation
refers to Jesus Christ
Heb. 5:9
23. Author of Life (or Prince of Life)
refers to Jesus Christ
Acts 3:15
24. Author of Peace
1 Corinthians 14:33
25. Hebrew transliteration: Avi
Meaning: "Father"
Psalm 68:5; Mal. 2
26. Hebrew transliteration: Avi-'ad
Meaning: "Everlasting Father," "Eternal Father"
Isaiah 9:6
27. Hebrew transliteration: Avinu
Meaning: "Our Father"
Isaiah 63:16
28. Hebrew transliteration: Avir Ya'akov
Meaning: "Mighty One of Jacob"
Isaiah 60:16
29. A Son over his own house
Hebrews 3:6 KJV
refers to Jesus Christ / The Church is Christ's house.
30. A Star out of Jacob
refers to the Messiah
Numbers 24:17 KJV
31. A stone of stumbling [to the unbeliever]
refers to the Messiah, Jesus Christ

Isaiah 8:14; 1 Peter 2:8
32. A sun and shield
Psa. 84:11
33. A very present help in trouble
Psa. 46:1
34. A witness to us
refers to Holy Spirit
Hebrews 10:15 KJV
35. Baptizer
refers to Holy Spirit
36. Bara' (Hebrew transliteration)
Meaning: "Creator"
Isa 40:28
37. Bara' Yisra'el (Hebrew transliteration)
Meaning: "Creator of Israel"
Isaiah 43:15
38. The Beginning
refers to Jesus Christ
Colossians 1:18
39. The Beginning and End
refers to Jehovah
Isaiah 41:4; 44:6; 48:12
"Alpha and Omega"
Rev. 1:8
40. Beginning of the creation of God
refers to Jesus Christ
Revelation 3:14 KJV
41. Beloved Son
refers to Jesus Christ
Col. 1:13-14
42. Blessed and only Potentate (or Blessed and only Ruler)

refers to Jesus Christ
1 Timothy 6:15
43. Blessed Hope
Titus 2:13
44. Branch
Zec. 6:12, 3:8, etc.
45. Bread of Life
refers to Jesus Christ
John 6:26-35; 47-48
46. Bread of God
refers to Jesus Christ
John 6:33
47. Bridegroom
refers to Jesus Christ
Matthew 25:1; Luke 5:34-35
The bride is the Church
Ephesians 5:27
48. Bright and morning star
refers to Jesus Christ
Rev. 22:16
49. Buckler to all those that trust in him
Psalm 18:30 KJV
50. Buckler to them that walk uprightly
Proverbs 2:7 KJV
51. By whom all things were made both in heaven and on earth
Nicene Creed
52. Captain of their salvation
refers to Jesus Christ
Hebrews 2:10
53. Chief Cornerstone
Greek: akrogoniaios akrogoniaios lithos

refers to Jesus Christ
Ephesians 2:20; 1 Peter 2:6
54. Christ
Meaning "the chosen one" or "the anointed one"
Greek: Χριστός
Greek transliteration: Khristos
Latin: Christus
Hebrew transliteration: mashiakh
Aramaic transliteration: mshikha—from which came the English word "Messiah"
55. Chief Shepherd
refers to Jesus Christ
1 Peter 5:4
56. Chosen of God
refers to Jesus Christ
Luke 23:35
57. Christ Jesus
Acts 19:4; Romans 3:24; 8:1; 1 Corinthians 1:2, 30; Hebrews 3:1; 1 Peter 5:10, 14
58. Christ Jesus our Lord
Romans 8:38-39
59. The Christ of God
Luke 9:20
60. Our Christ Passover
1 Corinthians 5:7
61. Christ the Lord
Luke 2:11
62. Christ the Power of God
1 Cor 1:23-24
63. Christ the power of God, and the wisdom of God

1 Cor 1:23-24
64. Christ in you, the hope of glory
Colossians 1:27 KJV
65. Christ the King of Israel
Mark 15:32 KJV
66. Comforter
refers to the Holy Spirit
John 14:16, 26; 15:26; 16:7 KJV
67. Confidence of all the ends of the Earth
Psalm 65:5 KJV
68. Confidence of them that are afar off upon the sea
Psalm 65:5 KJV
69. Consolation of Israel
Luke 2:25 KJV
refers to Jesus Christ
70. Consuming Fire
Hebrew transliteration: `akal `esh
Deuteronomy 4:24
Greek transliteration: katanalisko pur
Heb. 12:29
71. Cornerstone
Isaiah 28:16; Ephesians 2:20; 1 Peter 2:6
72. Counselor
Isaiah 9:6
73. Covenant of the people
refers to the Messiah
Isaiah 42:6; 49:8 KJV
74. Creator or The Creator
Hebrew transliteration: Boreh
Isaiah 40:28; John 1:3; Romans 1:25
75. Creator of Israel

Hebrew transliteration: bara' yisra'el
Isaiah 43:15
76. Creator of the ends of the Earth
Isaiah 40:28 KJV
77. Dayspring from on high
refers to Jesus Christ
Luke 1:78 KJV, NKJV, ASV, DARBY, GNV
NLV: "a light from heaven will shine on us"
NASB: "the Sunrise from on high"
HCSB: "the Dawn from on high"
TLB: "heaven's dawn is about to break upon us" CEV: "God's love and kindness will shine upon us like the sun that rises in the sky."
78. Daystar or Day Star
2 Peter 1:19 KJV
NKJV, NASB, ESV: "Morning Star"
79. Deliverer
refers to Jesus Christ
Romans 11:26
80. Desire of All Nations
refers to Jesus Christ
Haggai 2:7 KJV
81. Greek transliteration: Despotes
Meaning: "Master"
Luke 2:29; Acts 4:24; 2 Peter 2:1; Jude 4; Rev. 6:10
82. The Door
John 10:9
refers to Jesus Christ
83. Door of the sheep
refers to Jesus Christ
John 10:7

84. Greek: Dunastes
Meaning: "Potentate," "Sovereign"
1 Timothy 6:15

85. Dwelling Place
Psalm 90:1
Hebrew transliteration: Ma'on or Ma'own

86. Ancient Aramaic (Leeshana Ateeqah) transliteration: Eashoa Msheekha
This is the name "Jesus Christ" in Ancient Aramaic, a language He spoke while on Earth.
Eashoa = Jesus / Msheekha = Christ

87. Hebrew transliteration: Ehyeh asher ehyeh
Meaning: "I Am that I Am"
Exodus 3:14
Modern Hebrew translitation: Ehiyeh sh'Ehiyeh

88. Hebrew transliteration: `El
generic word for "god"

89. Hebrew transliteration: El Ah or Elah
Compare: Allah

90. Hebrew transliteration: Elayuth

91. Hebrew transliteration: El Berith

92. Hebrew transliteration: El Elohe Yisrael
Meaning: "El, the God of Israel"

93. Hebrew transliteration: El `Elyon
Meaning: "Most High God"

94. Hebrew transliteration: El Gibhor
Meaning: "The Mighty God"
Isaiah 9:6

95. Hebrew transliteration: `Eloah—interchangeable with Elohim

Aramaic transliteration: Ĕlāhā
96. Hebrew transliteration: Elohai or Elohei
Meaning: "My God" or "God of" —as in Elohai Avraham—"God of Abraham"
97. Hebrew transliteration: `Elohiym or Elohim or Aleim
Genesis 1:1; Exodus 3:1, etc.
98. Hebrew transliteration: El Olam
99. Greek transliteration: Eloi (elói)
Greek: Ἐλωΐ
Derived from Aramaic/Syriac: Eil or elah (transliterations) —meaning: "He Is"
Mark 15:34 KJV
100. Hebrew transliteration: El Roi
101. Hebrew transliteration: El Shaddai
Meaning: "God Almighty"
102. Hebrew transliteration: `Elyown, `Elyown, `Elohiym, `Elyon
Meaning: "The Most High God"
Genesis 14:18-20, 22; Psa. 78:56
103. Hebrew transliteration: Esh okhlah
Meaning: "Consuming Fire"
Deuteronomy 4:24
104. The Eternal Life —refers to Jesus Christ
John 1:1-2; 6:40
105. Hebrew transliteration: `Even Yisrael
Meaning: "Stone of Israel"
Genesis 49:24
106. Everlasting Father (or Eternal Father)
Isaiah 9:6
107. Everlasting God
Hebrew transliteration: `Owlam `El—Gene-

sis 21:33

Hebrew transliteration: `Owlam `Elohiym — Isa 40:28

Greek: Aionios Theos — Romans 16:26

108. Everlasting King
Jeremiah 10:10; 1 Timothy 1:16-17

109. Faithful and True
refers to Jesus Christ
Revelation 19:11, 13

110. Faithful Creator
1 Peter 4:19 KJV

111. Faithful Witness
refers to Jesus Christ
Rev. 1:5

112. Father

113. Father of glory
Ephesians 1:17 KJV

114. Father of lights
James 1:17

115. Father of mercies
2 Corinthians 1:3 KJV

116. Father of the fatherless
Psa. 68:5

117. Father of our Lord Jesus Christ
Romans 15:6; 2 Corinthians 1:3; 11:31; Ephesians 3:14, Colossians 1:3; 1 Peter 1:3 KJV

118. Father of spirits
Hebrews 12:9 KJV

119. Father to Israel
Jeremiah 31:9

120. The First and the Last
Isaiah 44:6, 48:12

121. First begotten of the dead
Revelation 1:5 KJV
refers to Jesus Christ
122. Firstborn of All Creation
Col. 1:15-16
refers to Jesus Christ
123. Firstborn of Many Brothers (or Firstborn among many brethren)
Romans 8:29
refers to Jesus Christ
124. Firstborn from among the dead
Col. 1:18
refers to Jesus Christ
125. Firstborn of every creature
refers to Jesus Christ
Colossians 1:15 KJV
126. Former of all things
Jeremiah 10:16; 51:19 KJV
127. Foundation
Meaning: "a Sure Foundation"
Isaiah 28:16 KJV
128. Fountain of Living Waters
Jeremiah 2:13; 7:13 — compare Rev. 7:17
129. Fullness of the Godhead bodily
refers to Jesus Christ
Col. 2:9
130. Hebrew transliteration: Gaol
131. Glorious LORD
Isaiah 33:21
132. Glory of their strength
Psalm 89:17 KJV
133. Glory of thy people Israel

refers to Jesus Christ
Luke 2:32 KJV

134. God—written "G-d" by pious Jews and some Christians

135. God Almighty
Genesis 28:3; 35:11; 43:14; 48:3; Exodus 6:3; Revelation 4:8; 11:17; 15:3; 16:7; 16:14; 21:22 KJV

136. God alone
Psalm 86:10 KJV

137. God and Father of all
Ephesians 4:6 KJV

138. God and Father of our Lord Jesus Christ
2 Corinthians 11:31; Ephesians 1:3; 1 Peter 1:3 KJV
2 Corinthians 11:31; Ephesians 1:3; 1 Peter 1:3 KJV

139. God full of compassion
Psa. 86:15

140. God most high
Psa. 57:2; Luke 8:28

141. Godhead
Acts 17:29; Col. 2:9; Romans 1:20

142. God my maker
Job 35:10 KJV

143. God of Abraham
Hebrew transliteration: Elohei Avraham
Genesis 26:24, 28:13; Exodus 3:6; 1 Chronicles 29:18; Psalm 47:9; Matthew 22:32; Mark 12:26; Acts 3:13; etc.

144. God of Abraham, God of Isaac, and God of Jacob
Hebrew transliteration: Elohei Avraham,

Elohei Yitzchak ve Elohei Ya`aqov

Exodus 3:6, 15-16; Matthew 22:32; Luke 20:37; Acts 3:13; 7:32; etc.

145. God of all comfort
2 Corinthians 1:3 KJV

146. God of all flesh
Jeremiah 32:27 KJV

147. God of all grace
1 Peter 5:10 KJV

148. God of all the families of Israel
Jeremiah 31:1 KJV

149. God of Isaac
Hebrew transliteration: Elohei Yitzchak
Genesis 28:13; Exodus 3:6; 4:5; Matthew 22:32; Mark 12:26; Luke 20:37; Acts 7:32

150. God of me
said by Jesus Christ of the Father, as He hung on the cross
Greek: Θεέ μου
Matthew 27:46
Literal translation: "God of me" (Interlinear Bible)
KJV, NKJV, NASB, and ESV say "My God"

151. God of Sarah, God of Rebecca, God of Leah, God of Rachel
Hebrew transliteration: Elohei Sara, Elohei Rivka, Elohei Leah ve Elohei Rakhel

152. God of the Covenant

153. God of your fathers
Exodus 3:13, 15; etc.

154. God of glory
Psalm 29:3; Acts 7:2 KJV

155. God of gods
Deuteronomy 10:17; Joshua 22:22; Psalm 136:2; Daniel 2:47; 11:36 KJV

156. God of heaven
Genesis 24:3; 24:7; 2 Chronicles 36:23; Ezra 1:2; Nehemiah 1:4-5; Psalm 136:26; Daniel 2:18-19; Jonah 1:9; Revelation 11:13; 16:11; etc.

157. God of heaven and Earth

158. God of hope

159. God of Israel

160. God of Jacob

161. Hebrew transliteration: God of Jeshurun (or Yeshurun)
Hebrew: Jeshurun
Literal meaning: God of the upright
"Jeshurun" is a poetic name for Israel
Deuteronomy 33:26 KJV

162. God of knowledge

163. God of love and peace

164. God of my life

165. God of my mercy

166. God of my praise

167. God of my righteousness

168. God of my rock

169. God of our salvation

170. God of patience and consolation

171. God of peace

172. God of the armies of Israel

173. God of the living

174. God of the spirits of all flesh

175. God of the whole Earth

176. God of thy fathers

177. God of truth and without iniquity
178. God only wise
179. God our Rock
Deuteronomy 32:4
180. God our Savior
Titus 3:3-5
181. God our shield
Psalm 84:9 KJV
182. God ready to pardon
183. God that answereth by fire
184. God, that cannot lie
see: truth
185. God, that comforteth those that are cast down
186. God that doest wonders
Psalm 77:14 KJV
187. God that formed thee
188. God, that giveth to all men liberally
189. God that judgeth in the Earth
190. God that made the world and all things therein
191. God that performeth all things for me
192. God that showeth mercy
193. God the Father
194. God, the Father Almighty, Maker of all things visible and invisible
Nicene Creed
195. God, the Father Almighty, Maker of heaven and earth, and of all things visible and invisible
Niceno-Constantinopolitan Creed
196. God the Hero

Hebrew transliteration: El ha-Gibbor

197. God the Judge of all
198. God the LORD
199. God, which always causeth us to triumph in Christ
200. God, which doeth great things and unsearchable; marvelous things without number
201. God which fed me all my life long unto this day
Genesis 48:15 KJV
202. God, which giveth us the victory through our Lord Jesus Christ
203. God, which hath not turned away my prayer
204. God which raiseth the dead
205. God, which trieth our hearts
1 Thessalonians 2:4 KJV
206. The God Who Sees
Genesis 16:13
207. Good Shepherd
refers to Jesus Christ
John 10:11, 14-15
208. God's servant
refers to Jesus Christ
209. God's righteous servant
refers to Jesus Christ
210. Governor among the nations
Psalm 22:28 KJV
211. Gracious and merciful God
Exodus 34:6; 2 Chronicles 30:9; Nehemiah 9:17; 9:31; Psalm 116:5; Joel 2:13; Jonah 4:2
212. Great High Priest

Heb. 4:14
213. Great King above all gods
Psalm 95:3 KJV
214. Great King over all the Earth
Psalm 47:2 KJV
215. Great Shepherd of the Sheep
Heb. 13:20 — refers to Jesus Christ
216. Habitation of Justice
Jeremiah 31:23; 50:7
217. Hebrew transliteration: ha'El Elohe abi-ka
   Meaning: "El the God of your father"
218. Hebrew transliteration: ha'Elohiym
   Meaning: "The Trinity" — consisting of the Father, Yeshua, and Ruach haQodesh
219. Hebrew transliteration: HaKadosh or Hakkadosh
   Meaning: "The Holy One"
   Isaiah 40:24
220. Hebrew transliteration: Hamelekh Ha-goel
   Meaning: "The Redeeming Angel"
   Genesis 48:16
221. Hebrew transliteration: HaShem
   Meaning: "the Name"
222. Head of the Church / Head of the Body, the Church
   refers to Jesus Christ
   Eph 1:22; 5:23; Col. 1:18
223. Health of my countenance
224. Heavenly Father
225. Heir of all things

refers to Jesus Christ
Heb. 1:2, 14-21

226. Helper of the fatherless
Psalm 10:14 KJV
NASB: Helper of the orphan

227. He in whom I trust

228. He Is
said by Jesus Christ of the Father, as He hung on the cross, and by Jacob after God's communication to him in Genesis

Mark 15:34 KJV as Greek transliteration: "Eloi"

Original Greek: Ἐλωϊ

Derived from Aramaic: Eil or elah (transliterations) —meaning: "He Is"

Many translations say "My God"

229. He that abideth of old
Psalm 55:19 KJV
NKJV: He who abides from of old
NCV: God who lives forever
NASB: The One who sits enthroned from of old
NIV: God, who is enthroned from of old, who does not change

230. He that built all things
Hebrews 3:4 KJV
NKJV: He who built all things
ESV, NASB, NRSV: The builder of all things

231. He that by wisdom made the heavens
Psalm 136:5 KJV
NKJV: Him who by wisdom made the heavens

NASB: Him who made the heavens with skill

232. He that called you into the grace of Christ

233. He that calleth you
1 Thessalonians 5:24 KJV
ESV, NASB, RSV: He who calls you

234. He that cometh from above
refers to Jesus Christ

235. He that cometh from heaven
refers to Jesus Christ

236. He that cometh in the name of the Lord
refers to the Messiah, Jesus Christ
Psalm 118:26; Matthew 21:9; 23:39; Mark 11:9; Luke 13:35 KJV
ASV, Darby: "He that cometh in the name of Jehovah"
NKJV, ESV: "He who comes in the name of the Lord"
NASB: "The One who comes in the name of the LORD"
NOG: "The one who comes in the name of Yahweh"
WEB: "He who comes in Yahweh's name"
CJB: "He who comes in the name of Adonai"

237. He that comforteth you
Isaiah 51:12 KJV
NKJV: "He who comforts you"

238. He that createth the wind
Amos 4:13 KJV
NKJV, NASB: "creates the wind"

239. He that declareth unto man what is his

thought
Amos 4:13 KJV
NKJV: "Who declares to man what his thought is"
ESV: "…declares to man what is his thought"
NASB: "…declares to man what are His thoughts"

240. He that doth speak
Isaiah 52:6 KJV
NKJV: Therefore My people shall know My name; Therefore they shall know in that day That I am He who speaks: 'Behold, it is I.'"
NASB: Therefore My people shall know My name; therefore in that day I am the one who is speaking, 'Here I am.'"

241. He that endured such contradiction of sinners against himself
Hebrews 12:3 KJV
NASB: Him who has endured such hostility by sinners against Himself
NIV: Him who endured such opposition from sinners

242. He that filleth all in all
Ephesians 1:23 KJV
NKJV, NASB, ESV: "Him who fills all in all"

243. He that formed thee from the womb
Isaiah 44:24 KJV
NKJV: "He who formed you from the womb"
NASB: "The One who formed you from the womb"

244. He that formeth the mountains
Amos 4:13 KJV

NASB: He who forms mountains

245. He that giveth breath unto the people

246. He that giveth strength and power unto his people

247. He that has called us to glory and virtue
2 Peter 1:3 KJV

NKJV: "Him who called us by glory and virtue"

NASB: "…who called us by His own glory and excellence"

ESV: "Him who called us to his own glory and excellence"

248. He that hath mercy on them

249. He that hath the key of David
refers to Jesus Christ

250. He that hath the seven Spirits of God

251. He that holdeth the seven stars in his right hand

252. He that is able to do exceeding abundantly above all that we ask or think

253. He that is able to keep you from falling
Jude 1:24 KJV

ESV, NASB, NIV, NKJV: Him who is able to keep you from stumbling

254. He that is able to present you faultless before the presence of his glory

255. He that is from the beginning

256. He that is higher than the highest

257. He that is holy

258. He that is mighty

259. He that is of power to stablish you
Romans 16:25 KJV

NASB, NIV, NKJV: Him who is able to establish you
260. He that is true
261. He that judgeth me
262. He that judgeth righteously
1 Peter 2:23 KJV
NASB, NKJV: Him who judges righteously
ESV, NIV: Him who judges justly
263. He that keepeth Israel
264. He that keepeth thee
Psalm 121:3 KJV
ESV, NASB, NKJV, NRSV: He who keeps you
265. He that keepeth thy soul
Proverbs 24:12 KJV
NKJV, NASB: He who keeps your soul
ESV: He who keeps watch over your soul
NIV: He who guards your life
NOG: The One who guards your soul
266. He that liveth and was dead
refers to Jesus Christ
267. He that liveth for ever and ever
268. He that loved us
269. He that maketh the morning darkness
Amos 4:13 KJV
NASB: He who makes dawn into darkness
270. He that maketh the seven stars and Orion
Amos 5:8 KJV
NASB: "He who made the Pleiades and Orion"
271. He that made great lights

Psalm 136:7; Genesis 1:16 KJV
NKJV: "Him who made great lights"
NASB, LEB: "Him who made the great lights"
GNT, ICB, NCV: "He made the sun and the moon"

272. He that ministereth to you the Spirit
Galatians 3:5 KJV
NASB: "He who provides you with the Spirit"

273. He that openeth, and no man shutteth; and shutteth, and no man openeth

274. He that pondereth the heart
Proverbs 24:12 KJV, GNV
ESV, NIV: "He who weighs the heart"
CJB: "He who weighs hearts"
ERV: "The Lord knows everything, and he knows why you do things."
CEV: "God can read your mind. He watches each of us and knows our thoughts."

275. He that raised up Jesus from the dead

276. He that revealeth secrets
Daniel 2:28-29 KJV, ASV

AMPC, CJB, TLB, MEV: "He Who reveals secrets"
NOG: "The one who reveals secrets" ISV: "the Revealer of Secrets"
NASB, ESV: "He who reveals mysteries"
NIV, CSB, CEB, LEB, MSG, NRSV: "the Revealer of Mysteries"

277. He that rideth upon the heavens of heavens

278. He that sanctifieth
279. He that searcheth the hearts
280. He that shall come
refers to Jesus Christ
281. He that shall have dominion
refers to Jesus Christ
282. He that sitteth in the heavens
283. He that sitteth upon the circle of the Earth
284. He that sitteth upon the throne
285. He that smote Egypt in their firstborn
286. He that spared not his own Son (the Father
287. He that speaketh from heaven
288. He that strengtheneth the spoiled against the strong
289. He that stretched out the Earth above the waters
290. He that took me out of the womb
291. He that treadeth upon the high places of the Earth
292. He that turneth the shadow of death into the morning
293. He that washed us from our sins
refers to Jesus Christ
294. He that works miracles among you
Galatians 3:5
295. He which baptizeth with the Holy Ghost
refers to Jesus Christ
296. He which divided the Red Sea into parts
297. He which giveth life unto the world
298. He which hath anointed us

299. He which hath the sharp sword with two edges

300. He which is, and which was, and which is to come

Rev. 1:4; 8

301. He which is perfect in knowledge

Job 37:16-17

302. He which led his people through the wilderness

303. He which searcheth the reins and hearts

304. He which smote great kings

Psa. 136:17

305. He which stablisheth us with you in Christ

306. He which was ordained of God to be the Judge of quick and dead

refers to Jesus Christ

307. He who alone doeth great wonders

308. He who built the house

refers to Jesus Christ

Heb. 3:3

309. He who hath called you out of darkness into his marvelous light

310. He who has eyes like a flame of fire

Rev. 1:14-15; 2:18

311. He who walks in the midst of the seven golden candlesticks

Rev. 2:1

312. He who works all things after the counsel of his own will

Ephesians 1:11

313. He whom God hath sent

refers to Jesus Christ
314. He with whom we have to do
315. Highest
Matthew 21:9
316. High Priest (or Chief Priest)
refers to Jesus Christ
Hebrews 2:17; 3:1; 4:14-15; 6:20; 7:26; 8:1; 9:11
317. High priest of good things to come
refers to Jesus Christ
Heb. 9:11
318. High priest over the house of God
refers to Jesus Christ
Heb. 10:21
319. High priest forever after the order of Melchizedek
refers to the Messiah, Jesus Christ
Psalm 110:4
320. Him that ought to be feared
Psalm 76:11 KJV
NKJV: "Him who ought to be feared"
NASB, ESB: "Him who is to be feared"
NIV: "The One to be feared"
See: The fear of the Lord
321. His Anointed
refers to the Messiah, Jesus Christ)
See: Messiah and Christ
322. His dear Son
refers to Jesus Christ
Col. 1:13
323. His Son from heaven
refers to Jesus Christ
324. His Spirit that dwelleth in you

325. His unspeakable gift
refers to Jesus Christ
2 Corinthians 9:15 KJV
326. Holy God
Joshua 24:19
327. Holy One
Job 6:10; Psa. 16:10
328. Holy One of Israel
2 Ki. 19:22; Psa. 71:22, 78:41, etc.
329. Holy Ghost
Matthew 1:18, etc.
330. Holy Spirit
Luke 11:13, etc.
331. Holy Spirit of promise
332. Hope of Israel
refers to Jesus Christ
333. Hope of Israel, the Savior thereof in time of trouble
334. Horn of my salvation
335. House of defense
336. Greek transliteration: Hupsistos
Meaning: "Highest"
Matthew 21:9
337. Greek transliteration: Hupsistos Hupsistos Theos
Meaning: "The Most High God"
Mark 5:7; Acts 16:17; Heb. 7:1
338. I Am
John 8:58; Exodus 3:14
339. I AM THAT I AM
Exodus 3:14
Hebrew transliteration: Ehyeh asher ehyeh

Modern Hebrew translitation: Ehiyeh sh'Ehiyeh

340. I am a father to Israel
341. I am a great King
342. I am alive for evermore
refers to Jesus Christ
343. I am Alpha and Omega
refers to Jesus Christ
344. I am for you
345. I am from above
refers to Jesus Christ
346. I am God
347. I am God Almighty
348. I am gracious
349. I am he
350. I am he that comforteth you
351. I am he that doth speak
352. I am he that liveth, and was dead
refers to Jesus Christ
353. I am he which searcheth the reins and hearts
refers to Jesus Christ
354. I am holy
355. I am in the midst of Israel
356. I am married unto you
357. I am meek and lowly in heart
refers to Jesus Christ
358. I am merciful
359. I am the Almighty God
360. I am the bread of life
refers to Jesus Christ
361. I am the door

refers to Jesus Christ
362. I am the door of the sheep
refers to Jesus Christ
363. I am the first and the last
364. I am the God of Abraham, and the God of Isaac, and the God of Jacob
365. I am the God of thy fathers
366. I am the good shepherd
refers to Jesus Christ
367. I am the light of the world
refers to Jesus Christ
368. I am the living bread
refers to Jesus Christ
369. I am the LORD
370. I am the LORD, and there is none else
371. I am the Lord GOD
372. I am the LORD in the midst of the Earth
373. I am the LORD that doth sanctify you
374. I am the LORD that healeth thee
375. I am the LORD that maketh all things
376. I am the LORD that smiteth
377. I am the LORD, the God of all flesh
378. I am the LORD thy God
379. I am the LORD thy God from the land of Egypt
380. I am the LORD thy God that divideth the sea
381. I am the LORD thy God which leadeth thee by the way that thou shouldest go
382. I am the LORD thy God which teacheth thee to profit
383. I am the LORD which exercise lov-

ing-kindness, judgment, and righteousness
384. I am the LORD which hallow you
385. I am the LORD, your Holy One
386. I am the resurrection, and the life
refers to Jesus Christ
387. I am the root and offspring of David
refers to Jesus Christ
388. I am the Son of God
refers to Jesus Christ
389. I am the Vine
refers to Jesus Christ
390. I am The Way, The Truth, and The Life
refers to Jesus Christ
391. I am their inheritance ("their" refers to the priests)
392. I am thy exceeding great reward
393. I am thy part and thine inheritance ("thy" and "thine" refers to the Levites
394. I am thy salvation
395. I am thy Savior
396. I am thy shield
Genesis 15:1 KJV
397. I am with thee
Genesis 26:24; Acts 18:10; etc. KJV
NKJV, NASB, ESV: "I am with you"
398. I am with thee to deliver thee
Jeremiah 1:8 KJV
NKJV, NASB, ESV: "I am with you to deliver you"
399. I am with thee to save thee
Jeremiah 15:20 KJV
NASB: "I am with you to save you"

400. I am with you always
refers to Jesus Christ
Matthew 28:20

401. `Illay `Illay `Elahh ("The Most High God")
Dan. 5:18, 21

402. Image of the invisible God
refers to Jesus Christ

403. Immanuel
refers to Jesus Christ
Meaning: "God with us"
Matthew 1:20-23; Isaiah 7:14

404. I that speak in righteousness, mighty to save
Isaiah 63:1

405. Jah

406. Jealous
Hebrew transliteration: Qanna'
Exodus 34:14

407. Jealous God
Hebrew transliteration: Qanna' `El
Exodus 20:5; Deuteronomy 4:24, etc.

zzz

408. Hebrew transliteration: Yahweh M'Kaddesh or Jehovah M'Kaddesh
Meaning: Jehovah sanctifies
Leviticus 20:8, etc.

409. Hebrew transliteration: Jehovah or Yahweh or YHWH—the most often used name for God in the Hebrew Bible (appearing several thousand times) / It appears first in Genesis.

410. Hebrew transliteration:Jehovah `Elohi-

ym or Jehovah Elohim Genesis 3:23, etc.

411. Hebrew transliteration: Jehovah-Jireh

412. Hebrew transliteration: Jehovah-Mekoddishkem
Meaning: "The Lord who sanctifies you"
Leviticus 20:8 KJV

413. Hebrew transliteration: Jehovah-Nissi or YHWH-Nissi or Yahweh-Nissi
Meaning: "The LORD our Banner"
Exodus 17:8-15

414. Hebrew transliteration: Jehovah-Ra'ah
Meaning: "The Lord is my Shepherd"
Psa. 23:1

415. Hebrew transliteration: Jehovah-Rapha or YHWH-Rapha
Meaning: "The Lord that Healeth"
Exodus 15:26

416. Hebrew transliteration: Jehovah-Rohi

417. Hebrew transliteration: Jehovah-Rophe

418. Hebrew transliteration: Jehovah-Sabaoth

419. Hebrew transliteration: Jehovah-Shalom

420. Hebrew transliteration: Jehovah-Shammah
Meaning: "The Lord is there"

421. Hebrew transliteration: Jehovah-Tsidkenu
Meaning: "The Lord our Righteousness"

422. Hebrew transliteration: Je-Hoshua
Meaning: "Jehovah is Salvation"

423. English: Jesus—Salvation, or "the Lord

is salvation," "the Lord Saves"

French, Norman: Jésus

Greek: Ἰησοῦς

Greek transliteration: Iesous or Iēsoûs

Aramaic transliteration: yeshuu☉

This name appears many times in the Hebrew version of the Old Testament.

Note: Yeshua is an alternate form of Yehoshua or Y'hoshua (Joshua) or Jeshua

Hebrew transliteration: Yeshua—This name is preferred by many Messianic Jews.

Roman Latin: Iesvs

Late Latin: Iesus

424. Jesus Christ

425. Jesus Christ our Lord

426. Jesus Christ our Savior

Titus 3:5-7

427. Jesus Christ the righteous

428. Jesus of Nazareth (or Jesus the Nazarene) (Nazoraios

429. Jesus of Galilee (or Jesus the Galilean)

Matthew 26:69

430. Jesus the mediator of the new covenant

431. Jesus, thou Son of God most high

432. Jesus, which delivered us from the wrath to come

433. Joshua

Meaning: "Jehovah is Salvation"

434. The Judge

435. Judge of all the Earth

436. Judge of quick and dead

refers to Jesus Christ

437. Judge of the widows
Psa. 68:5
438. A just God and a Saviour
Isaiah 45:21
439. Just One
Isaiah 26:7; Acts 7:52; 22:14
440. Hebrew transliteration: Kadosh
441. Hebrew transliteration: Kanna
442. Greek transliteration: Katanalisko Pur
Meaning: "Consuming Fire"
Heb. 12:29
443. The King
444. King forever and ever
445. King of all the Earth
446. The King of Glory
Psalm 24:7-10
447. King of Heaven
448. King of Israel
2 Samuel 24:23; Psalm 98:6; Isaiah 6:5; Jeremiah 46:18; 48:15; 51:57
449. King of Kings
1 Timothy 6:15; Rev. 17:14, 19:16
Hebrew transliteration: Melech HaMelachim or Melech Malchei HaMelachim
Meaning: "The King, King of kings"
450. KING OF KINGS, AND LORD OF LORDS
451. King of Nations
452. King of saints
453. King of the Jews
refers to Jesus Christ
454. Greek transliteration: Ktizo

Meaning: "Creator"
Romans 1:25

455. Hebrew transliteration: Kokhav mi-ya'akov — Star from Jacob
Numbers 24:17

456. Greek transliteration: Kurios — "Lord", "Master"
Ephesians 6:9; Col. 4:1

457. Greek transliteration: Kurios Theos Pantokrator
Meaning: "Lord God Almighty"
Rev. 4:8, 11:17, 15:3, 16:7, 21:22

458. Lamb of God
refers to Jesus Christ

459. Lamb Slain Before the Foundation of the World
Rev. 13:8

460. The Life

461. Light of Israel
Isaiah 10:17; Psalm 27:1

462. Light of the Gentiles
refers to Jesus Christ — Luke 2:32

463. Light of the Nations
Isaiah 42:6
Hebrew transliteration: 'Or Goyim

464. Light of the world
John 8:12, 9:5

465. Light to lighten the Gentiles (a light to bring revelation to the Gentiles)
Luke 2:32

466. Lion of the tribe of Judah
refers to Jesus Christ

467. Living stone
1 Peter 2:4
468. Greek transliteration: Logos
Meaning: "The Word," "The Word of God"
John 1:1; Rev. 19:13
469. LORD
470. Lord also of the sabbath
471. Lord and Christ
472. Lord and Savior Jesus Christ
2 Peter 3:17-18
473. LORD God (Yehovah `Elohiym—Genesis 2:4, 3:23, etc.
474. Lord God Almighty
Greek: kurios theos pantokrator
Rev. 4:8, 11:17, 15:3, 16:7, 21:22
475. LORD God of Abraham, Isaac, and Israel
476. LORD God of gods
Joshua 22:22
Hebrew transliteration: Yehovah `El `Elohiym Yehovah
477. LORD God of Israel
478. LORD God of my salvation
479. LORD God of our fathers
480. LORD God of recompense
481. LORD God of the Hebrews
482. Lord God of the holy prophets
Revelation 22:6 KJV
483. LORD God of truth
484. LORD of hosts (or "Lord of the hosts")
Hebrew transliteration: yehovah tsaba' or Jehovah Sabaoth

appears 245 times in the Old Testament, including: 1 Samuel 1:3, 4:4; 1 Chronicles 11:9; Psa. 24:10; Isaiah 1:9; Mal. 4:3

485. Lord of Lords

Deuteronomy 10:17; Psa. 136:3; 1 Tim 6:15; Rev. 17:14, 19:16

486. Lord God of Your Fathers

appears in— Joshua 18:3; Deuteronomy 1:11, etc.

487. Lord God omnipotent

488. Lord GOD which gathereth the outcasts of Israel

489. Lord, holy and true

490. Lord Jesus

491. Lord Jesus Christ, the Son of God, begotten of the Father [the only-begotten; that is, of the essence of the Father, God of God,] Light of Light, very God of very God, begotten, not made, being of one substance with the Father

appears in— Nicene Creed

492. LORD most high

493. Lord of all

refers to Jesus Christ

494. Lord of glory

495. Lord of kings

496. Lord of lords

497. Lord of peace

498. Lord of the harvest

Matthew 9:38

499. The LORD our Peace

Hebrew transliteration: YHWH-Shalom

Judges 6:24

500. Lord of Sabaoth (or Tsabaoth)
Hebrew transliteration: Jehovah Sabaoth
501. Lord of the whole Earth
Micah 4:13
502. LORD on high
503. LORD our God
504. LORD our Lord
505. Lord, which art, and wast, and shalt be
Revelation 16:5
506. Love
Meaning: "God is love")
1 John 4:8, 16
507. Hebrew transliteration: Machseh
Meaning: "Fortress," "Shelter," "Refuge"
Psalm 91:2
508. Hebrew transliteration: Magen
509. Majesty on high
510. Man of sorrows, and acquainted with grief
refers to the Messiah
Isaiah 53:3
511. Man of war
Exodus 15:3; Isaiah 42:13
512. Hebrew transliteration: Ma'on
Meaning: "Refuge," "Dwelling place"
Psalm 90:1
513. Master
refers to Jesus Christ
Ephesians 6:9; Col. 4:1
Greek transliteration: kurios didaskalos
John 13:14, 20:16

514. Master of the World
Hebrew transliteration: Adon Olam or Ribbono shel `Olam

515. Mediator of a better covenant
refers to Jesus Christ

516. Mediator of the new testament
refers to Jesus Christ
Hebrews 9:15

517. Hebrew transliteration: Melekh

518. Hebrew transliteration: Melekh HaKavod
Meaning: "The King of Glory"—Psalm 24:7-10

519. Hebrew transliteration: Melekh Yisrael
Meaning: "King of Israel"
2 Samuel 24:23; Psalm 98:6; Isaiah 6:5; Jeremiah 46:18; 48:15; 51:57

520. Merciful and faithful high priest
Heb. 2:17

521. Merciful God
Deuteronomy 4:31; Neh. 9:31

522. Hebrew transliteration: Messiah or Meshiach or mashiakh
Meaning: "The Anointed One" or "The Chosen One"
Aramaic transliteration: mshikha
Greek equivalent (transliteration): Khristos—Christ

523. Mighty
Deuteronomy 10:17, etc.

524. Mighty God
Isaiah 9:6

525. Mighty God of Jacob
Genesis 49:24, etc.
526. Mighty One of Israel
Isaiah 1:24; Isaiah 30:29
527. Mighty One of Jacob
Isaiah 49:26, 60:16
Hebrew transliteration: Avir Ya'akov
528. Mighty terrible one
refers to the Messiah
Jeremiah 20:11 KJV
NKJV: "a mighty, awesome One"
NIV: "a mighty warrior"
NRSV: "a dread warrior"
529. Mine elect
Isaiah 42:1; 45:4; 65:9, 22 KJV
530. Mine Holy One
Habakkuk 1:12 KJV
531. Minister of the sanctuary, and of the true tabernacle
Heb. 8:2
532. Greek transliteration: Misthapodotes
Meaning: "Rewarder" of them that diligently seek Him
Heb. 11:6
533. Morning Star
2 Peter 1:19 NKJV, NASB, ESV, etc.
KJV: "Day Star"
534. Most High
Greek transliteration: Hupsistos Hupsistos
Numbers 24:16; Deuteronomy 32:8; Psa. 9:2, etc.
Numbers 24:16; Deuteronomy 32:8; 2 Samu-

el 22:14; Psa. 9:2,
Acts 7:48, 16:17. etc.

535. Most High God
Hebrew transliteration: `Elyown `Elyown `elohiym
Genesis 14:18-20, 22; Psa. 78:56
Hebrew transliteration: `Illay `Illay `elahh
Dan. 5:18, 21
Greek transliteration: Hupsistos Hupsistos Theos
Mark 5:7; Acts 16:17; Heb. 7:1

536. Most Mighty

537. Most upright

538. My beloved
refers to Jesus Christ
Matthew 12:18

539. My beloved Son
refers to Jesus Christ
Mark 1:10-11

540. My buckler

541. My defense

542. My defense and refuge in the day of my trouble

543. My deliverer

544. My exceeding joy

545. My Father

546. My father's God

547. My [God's] firstborn, higher than the kings of the Earth
refers to Jesus Christ

548. My fortress

549. My friend

550. My glory
551. My God
552. My goodness
553. My help
554. My hiding place
555. My hiding place and my shield
556. My high tower
557. My hope
558. My hope in the day of evil
559. My judge
560. My King
561. My lamp
562. My love
563. My portion for ever
Psa. 73:26
564. My portion in the land of the living
Psa. 142:5
565. My praise
566. My Redeemer
567. My refuge
568. My refuge and my portion
569. My refuge in the day of affliction
570. My rock
571. My salvation
572. My Savior
573. My [God's] servant
refers to Jesus Christ
574. My [God's] servant David
refers to Jesus Christ
575. My shepherd
576. My shield
577. My song

578. My stay
579. My strength and power
580. My strength and song
581. My strong habitation, whereunto I may continually resort
582. My strong refuge
583. My strong rock
584. My trust from my youth
Psa. 71:5
585. Nail in a sure place
Isaiah 22:23
586. The Name—used in Leviticus 24:11 and by many modern Jews
587. One LORD
Deuteronomy 6:4; Zechariah 14:9
588. One mediator between God and men
refers to Jesus Christ
589. Only begotten of the Father
refers to Jesus Christ
590. Only begotten Son of God
refers to Jesus Christ
591. Hebrew transliteration: 'Or Goyim
Meaning: "Light of the Nations"
Isaiah 42:6
592. Hebrew transliteration: 'Or Yisrael
Meaning: "Light of Israel"
Isaiah 10:17; Psalm 27:1
593. Our Father
Hebrew transliteration: ... `Ab
Isaiah 63:16, 64:8
Greek transliteration: ... Pater
Mat. 6:9

594. Our Captain
595. Our dwelling place
596. Our Father
597. Our Father, our King
Hebrew transliteration: Avinu Malkeinu
598. Our Father which is in heaven
599. Our guide
600. Our lawgiver
601. Our life
602. Our Lord Jesus Christ
603. Our peace
604. Our potter
605. Our Savior Jesus Christ
606. Hebrew transliteration: Palet
607. Greek transliteration: Pantokrator
Meaning: "Almighty"
2 Corinthians 6:18, Revelation 19:6
608. Place of broad rivers and streams
Isaiah 33:21
609. Plant of Renown
Lterally, "A Plant of the Name
Ezek. 34:29
610. Great Physician
611. Pioneer and Perfecter of our Faith (or Author and Finisher
612. Portion of Jacob
613. Portion of mine inheritance and of my cup
614. Possessor of heaven and Earth
615. Only Potentate
refers to Jesus Christ
Greek transliteration: dunastes

Meaning "Ruler," "Sovereign"
1 Timothy 6:15
616. Precious corner stone
617. Priest upon his throne
Zec. 6:13
618. Prince
refers to Jesus Christ
Acts 5:31
619. Prince and Savior
refers to Jesus Christ
Acts 5:31
620. Prince of Life
refers to Jesus Christ
621. Prince of Peace (Sar Shalom—Isaiah 9:6
refers to Jesus Christ
622. Prince of princes
623. Prince of the kings of the Earth
624. Promise of the Father
refers to Holy Spirit)
625. Qanna' and Qanna' `El ("Jealous"—Exodus 34:14 / "Jealous God"—Exodus 20:5; Deuteronomy 4:24, etc.)
626. Hebrew transliteration: Rabbī or Rabbi
Meaning "teacher"
refers to Jesus Christ)
627. Redeemer
Job 19:25; Psa. 19:14; Jeremiah 50:34; etc.
628. Redeemer of Israel
629. Redeeming Angel (Hamelekh Hagoel)
Genesis 48:16
630. Refuge (Ma'on)
Psalm 90:1

631. Refuge for the oppressed
632. Refuge from the storm
633. Refuge in times of trouble
Psa. 9:9
634. Rewarder of them that diligently seek Him
Heb. 11:6
635. Righteous Branch
refers to Jesus Christ
636. Righteous Father
637. Righteous One
Proverbs 21:12; Isa 24:16; Acts 3:14, 7:52, 22:14; 1 John 2:1
638. Rivers of water in a dry place
639. Rock
640. Rock of His Salvation (Tsur Yeshuato)
Deuteronomy 32:15
641. Rock of Israel
Hebrew transliteration: Tsur Yisrael or Tzur Israel
2 Samuel 23:3
642. Rock of my refuge
643. Rock of my salvation
644. Rock of my strength
645. Rock of offence (to both the houses of Israel)
Meaning: "a stone to strike and a rock to stumble over" NASB
Isaiah 8:14; Romans 9:33; 1 Peter 2:8
646. Rod out of the stem of Jesse
Isaiah 11:1
647. Hebrew: Roeh

Meaning: "Shepherd"
Genesis 49:24; Psalm 23:1; 80:1
648. Root of David
refers to Jesus Christ
649. Root of Jesse
Isaiah 11:10; Romans 15:12
refers to Jesus Christ
650. Only Ruler
Greek transliteration: dunastes
refers to Jesus Christ
1 Timothy 6:15 CEV, NIV, DARBY, GW, ISV
651. Ruler in Israel
652. Hebrew transliteration: Sabaoth
653. Salvation of God
refers to Jesus Christ
654. Salvation of Israel
655. Sanctifier
656. Sar Shalom
Hebrew: shalom = peace
"Prince of Peace" — Isaiah 9:6
657. Saving strength of his anointed
658. Savior
Luke 2:11; John 4:42; Acts 5:31; 13:23; Ephesians 5:23; Philippians 3:20; 1 Timothy 1:1; 2:3; 4:10; 2 Timothy 1:10; Titus 1:3-4; 2:10, 13; 3:4; 6; 2 Peter 1:1
659. Savior of all men
refers to Jesus Christ
660. Savior of the world
refers to Jesus Christ
1 John 4:14
661. Seed of Abraham

refers to Jesus Christ
662. Shaddai (or Shadday)
Exodus 6:2-3
663. Shadow from the heat
Isaiah 25:4
664. Hebrew: Shaphat
665. Shelter for me, A
Psa. 61:3
666. Shepherd
Hebrew translitation: Roeh
Genesis 49:24; Psalm 23:1; 80:1
667. Shepherd of Israel
Hebrew transliteration: Ro'eh Yisra'el
668. Great Shepherd of the Sheep
Heb. 13:20
669. Shield
Meaning: "My Shield"
2 Samuel 22:3; Psa. 28:7, 119:114, 144:2
670. Hebrew transliteration: Shiloh
Meaning: "He whose it is" or "he who is to be sent," "that which belongs to him"
Refers to the Messiah
Genesis 49:10
671. Hebrew transliteration: Shaphat / Shofet
Meaning: "Judge"
Psalm 50:6
672. Shelter (for me)
Hebrew transliteration: Machaceh
Psa. 61:3
673. Shepherd and Bishop of your souls
674. Shepherd of Israel
675. Shield of Abraham

Hebrew: Magen Avraham
676. Shield of thy help
677. Son
678. Son of David
refers to Jesus Christ
679. Son of God
refers to Jesus Christ
680. Son of man
refers to Jesus Christ
681. Son of the Blessed
refers to Jesus Christ
682. Son of the Father
refers to Jesus Christ
683. Son of the Highest
refers to Jesus Christ
684. Son of the living God
refers to Jesus Christ
685. Greek transliteration: Sophia
Meaning: "The Wisdom of God"
686. Greek transliteration: Soter Meaning: "Savior"
687. Spirit of Christ
Greek transliteration: pneuma christos)
Romans 8:9; 1 Peter 1:11
688. Spirit of counsel and might
689. Spirit of glory and of God
690. Spirit of God
Hebrew transliteration: ruwach `elohiym
Genesis 1:2; 1 Samuel 10:10
Greek transliteration: pneuma theos
Romans 8:9
691. Spirit of Grace

Heb. 10:29
692. Spirit of Holiness
Romans 1:4
693. Spirit of knowledge and of the fear of the LORD
Isaiah 11:2
694. Spirit of Life
Rev. 11:11
695. Spirit of Mercy
696. Spirit of the living God
697. Spirit of the LORD
698. Spirit of Truth
John 14:17, 15:26, 16:13; 1 John 4:6
699. Spirit of wisdom and understanding
Ephesians 1:17; Isaiah 11:2
700. Stone
701. Stone, A tried
Isaiah 28:16
702. Stone of Israel
Hebrew tranliteration: 'Even Yisrael
Genesis 49:24
703. Stone of stumbling
Isaiah 8:14
704. Strength
Psa. 19:14, etc.
705. Strength of Israel
1 Samuel 15:29; Psa. 68:33-34; Joel 3:16; Micah 5:3-4
706. Strength to the needy in his distress, A
707. Strength to the poor, A
Isaiah 25:4
708. Strength of my heart

709. Strength of my salvation
710. Strong One
Hebrew transliteration: Adir
711. A strong LORD
Psalm 89:8 KJV
712. A strong tower from the enemy
Psalm 61:3 KJV
713. Stumblingstone
Romans 9:33; 1 Peter 2:8
714. Sun of Righteousness
Malachi 4:2
refers to Jesus Christ
715. Sword of thy excellency
Deuteronomy 33:29
716. Greek transliteration: Theos
Meaning: "God"
717. Greek transliteration: Theotes
Col. 2:9; Romans 1:20
718. That man whom He hath ordained
refers to Jesus Christ
719. The Almighty
Nicene Creed
720. The beginning and the ending
721. The beginning, the firstborn from the dead
refers to Jesus Christ
722. The Branch of righteousness
refers to Jesus Christ
723. The Breaker (as in, the Deliverer
Micah 2:13
724. The Bridegroom
refers to Jesus Christ

725. The brightness of His glory
refers to Jesus Christ
726. The chief corner stone
refers to Jesus Christ
727. The chief Shepherd
refers to Jesus Christ
728. The Christ
729. The Christ of God
Luke 9:20 KJV
730. The Comforter
refers to Holy Spirit
731. The Deliverer
refers to Jesus Christ
732. The earnest of our inheritance
refers to Holy Spirit
733. The eternal God
734. The eternal Spirit
735. The express image of his person
refers to Jesus Christ
736. The faithful and true witness
737. The faithful God
738. The Father almighty (from the Apostles' Creed
739. The fear of Isaac
740. The first and the last
741. The first-begotten
refers to Jesus Christ
742. The glorious LORD
743. The Godhead
744. The great and dreadful God
745. The great God
746. The great God that formed all things

747. The Great, the Mighty God
748. the great, the mighty, and the awesome God
Nehemiah 9:32 NASB
KJV: The great, the mighty, and the terrible God
"terrible" in KJV means "awesome"
Nehemiah 9:32 KJV
749. The Head
refers to Jesus Christ
750. The head of the corner
Matthew 21:42; Mark 12:10; Luke 20:17; Acts 4:11; 1 Peter 2:7 KJV
refers to Jesus Christ
751. The high and lofty One that inhabiteth eternity
Isaiah 57:15 KJV
752. The high God their redeemer
753. The Highest
754. The Holy
755. The Holy One
756. The Holy One, Blessed be He—phrase common among Jews
Hebrew transliteration: HaKadosh Baruch Hu or Hakodesh baruch hu or Hakodosh boruch hu
757. The Holy One and the Just
refers to Jesus Christ
Acts 3:14 KJV
758. The Holy One in the midst of thee
Hosea 11:9; 12:6 KJV
759. The Holy One of God

refers to Jesus Christ
760. Holy One of Israel
Hebrew transliteration: Kadosh Israel
761. The hope of their fathers
Jeremiah 50:7 KJV
762. The Husbandman
refers to the Father
John 15:1 KJV
763. The invisible God
764. The Just One
765. The King eternal, immortal, invisible
766. The Lamb
refers to Jesus Christ
767. The Lamb slain from the foundation of the world
refers to Jesus Christ
768. The Lamb that was slain
refers to Jesus Christ
769. The last Adam
refers to Jesus Christ
770. The lifter up of mine head
771. The Light
772. The light of the world
refers to Jesus Christ
John 8:12 KJV
773. The living bread which came down from heaven
refers to Jesus Christ
John 6:51 KJV
774. The living Father
775. The Living God
776. The Lord from heaven

refers to Jesus Christ

777. The LORD is present

Hebrew transliteration: YHWH-Shammah or Jehovah-shammah

Ezekiel 48:35

778. The LORD mighty in battle

Psalm 24:8

779. The LORD my banner

Hebrew transliteration: Yahweh-Nissi or Jehovah Nissi

Exodus 17:15 KJV

780. The LORD my strength

781. The LORD my Shepherd

Hebrew transliteration: YHWH-Ro'i

Psalm 23:1

782. The LORD our maker

783. The LORD our righteousness

Hebrew transliteration: YHWH-Tsidkenu

Jeremiah 23:6

784. The LORD strong and mighty

785. The LORD that doth sanctify you

786. The LORD that healeth thee

787. The LORD that is faithful

788. The LORD that maketh all things

789. The LORD that smiteth

790. The LORD the God

791. The LORD, the God of Hosts

792. The LORD the Judge

793. THE LORD THY GOD

794. The LORD thy God from the land of Egypt

795. The LORD thy God in the midst of thee

796. The LORD thy Redeemer
797. The LORD which hallows you
798. The LORD which will help thee
799. The LORD will provide
Hebrew transliteration: YHWH-Yireh or Jehovah-jireh
Genesis 22:13-14
800. The LORD your God which goeth before you
801. The Lord's Christ
refers to Jesus Christ
Luke 2:26 KJV
802. The Majesty in the heavens
Hebrews 8:1 KJV
803. The Messiah— refers to Jesus Christ
804. The Messiah the Prince
refers to Jesus Christ
Daniel 9:25 KJV
805. The mighty God
806. The Most High
807. The most high God
Genesis 14:18-20; Numbers 24:16; Psalm 46:4; 78:56, Daniel 3:26; Mark 5:7, Acts 16:17, etc. KJV
808. The Most High over all the Earth
Psalm 83:18 KJV
809. The Most Holy
refers to Jesus Christ
Daniel 9:24 KJV
810. The only Lord God
Jude 1:4 KJV
811. The only true God

John 17:3 KJV
812. The only wise God
1 Timothy 1:17; Romans 16:27 KJV
813. The only wise God our Savior
Jude 1:25; Romans 16:27 KJV
814. The pearl of great price
Matthew 13:46 KJV
NKJV, NASB, ESV: "One pearl of great value"
815. The Prophet
Matthew 21:11; John 7:40 KJV
refers to Jesus Christ
816. The propitiation for our sins
1 John 2:2; 4:10 KJV
refers to Jesus Christ
817. The resurrection, and the life
refers to Jesus Christ
John 11:25 KJV
818. The righteous judge
2 Timothy 4:8 KJV
819. The righteous LORD
Psalm 11:7 KJV
820. The Rock
2 Samuel 22:47; 23:3; Psalm 62:7; 89:26; 94:22, etc. KJV
821. The Rock that begat thee
Deuteronomy 32:18 KJV
NKJV, NASB: "The Rock who begot you"
ESV: "The Rock that bore you"
822. The rock that is higher than I
Psalm 61:2 KJV, NKJV, NASB
823. The root and the offspring of David

refers to Jesus Christ
Revelation 22:16 KJV, NKJV
NASB: "The root and the descendant of David"

824. The seven Spirits of God
refers to Holy Spirit
Revelation 3:1; 4:5; 5:6 KJV, NKJV, NASB

825. The shadow of a great rock in a weary land
Isaiah 32:2 KJV, NKJV
NASB: "Like the shade of a huge rock in a parched land"

826. The Son
refers to Jesus Christ
Matthew 4:6; 11:27; Mark 13:32 KJV—and numerous other verses

827. The Spirit
Genesis 1:2; 41:38; Exodus 31:3; 35:31; Numbers 11:25-26; 24:2; 27:18; Deuteronomy 34:9; Judges 3:10; 6:34; 11:29; 13:25; 14:6, 19; 15:14; 1 Samuel 10:6; Ecclesiastes 12:7; Isaiah 11:2; 40:13; Matthew 3:16; 4:1; Luke 4:14; Acts 8:39; Romans 8:26 KJV—and numerous other verses

828. The Spirit of his Son
refers to Holy Spirit
Galatians 4:6 KJV, NKJV, NASB, ESV

829. The Spirit of your Father
Matthew 10:20 KJV, NKJV, NASB, ESV

830. The stone which the builders disallowed
refers to Jesus Christ
1 Peter 2:7 KJV
NKJV, NASB: "The stone which the builders

rejected"
ESV: "The stone that the builders rejected"
831. The true bread from heaven
refers to Jesus Christ
John 6:32 KJV
832. The true God
2 Chronicles 15:3; Jeremiah 10:10; John 17:3;
1 Thessalonians 1:9; 1 John 5:20 KJV
833. The true light
refers to Jesus Christ
John 1:9; 1 John 2:8 KJV, NKJV, NASB, ESV
834. The uncorruptible God
Romans 1:23 KJV, NKJV, NASB
ESV: "The immortal God"
835. The way, the truth, and the life
refers to Jesus Christ
John 14:6 KJV
NKJV, NASB, ESV: "The way, and the truth, and the life"
836. The Word of Life
refers to Jesus Christ
1 John 1:1 KJV, NASB, ESV
837. Thine everlasting light
Isaiah 60:20 KJV
NKJV, ESV: "Your everlasting light"
NASB: "An everlasting light"
838. Thine Husband
refers to God as Israel's husband
Isaiah 54:5 KJV
NKJV, NASB, ESV: "Your husband"
839. Thou preserver of men
Job 7:20 KJV

NKJV, NASB: "You, O watcher of men"
ESV: "You watcher of mankind"
840. Thou that dwellest between the cherubim
Psalm 80:1; Isaiah 37:16 KJV
NKJV: "You who dwell between the cherubim"
NASB: "You who are enthroned above the cherubim"
ESV: "You who are enthroned upon the cherubim"
841. Thou that dwellest in the heavens
Psalm 123:1 KJV
NKJV: "You who dwell in the heavens"
NASB, ESV: "You who are enthroned in the heavens!"
842. Thou that hearest prayer
Psalm 65:2 KJV
NKJV, NASB, ESV: "You who hear prayer"
843. Thou that inhabitest the praises of Israel
Psalm 22:3 KJV
NASB: "You who are enthroned upon the praises of Israel"
844. Thou that leadest Joseph like a flock
Psalm 80:1 KJV
NKJV, NASB, ESV: "You who lead Joseph like a flock"
845. Thou that liftest me up from the gates of death
Psalm 9:13
NKJV, NASB, ESV: "You who lift me up from the gates of death"

846. Thou that savest by thy right hand
Psalm 17:7 KJV
NASB: "Savior of those who take refuge at Your right hand"
ESV: "Savior of those who seek refuge from their adversaries at your right hand"
NKJV: "You who save those who trust in You From those who rise up against them"

847. Thou whom my soul loveth
Song 1:7
NASB, ESV: "You whom my soul loves"
NKJV, NIV: "You whom I love"

848. True God
1 John 5:20 KJV, NASB
NKJV, ESV: "Him who is true"

849. Thy Creator
Ecclesiastes 12:1 KJV
NKJV, NASB, ESV: "Your Creator"

850. Thy exceeding great reward
Genesis 15:1 KJV
NKJV: "Your exceedingly great reward"

851. Thy Father that hath bought thee
Deuteronomy 32:6 KJV
NKJV: "Your Father, who bought you"
NASB: "Your Father who has bought you"

852. Thy God that pleadeth the cause of his people
Isaiah 51:22 KJV
NKJV, ESV: "Who pleads the cause of his people"
NASB: "Who contends for His people"

853. Thy good Spirit

Nehemiah 9:20; Psalm 143:10 KJV
NKJV, NASB, ESV: "Your good Spirit"
854. Thy holy child Jesus
Acts 4:27, 30 KJV
NKJV, NASB ESV: "Your holy servant"
855. Thy keeper
Psalm 121:5 KJV
NASB, ESV: "Your keeper"
856. Thy life, and the length of thy days
Deuteronomy 30:20 KJV
NASB: "Your life and the length of your days"
857. Thy Lord the LORD
Isaiah 51:22 KJV
NASB: "Your Lord, the Lord"
858. Thy Maker
Isaiah 51:13; 54:5; 45:9 KJV
NKJV, NASB, ESV: "Your Maker"
859. Thy shade upon thy right hand
Psalm 121:5 KJV
NASB: "…Your shade on your right hand"
860. Tower of salvation
2 Samuel 22:51 KJV
861. The Trinity—a word that does not appear in Scripture, but is used by Christians to refer to the One True God who is 3 persons: the Father, the Son, and the Holy Spirit
862. The True Vine
refers to Jesus Christ
John 15:1 KJV, NKJV
863. The Truth
Hebrew transliteration: Emet

864. Hebrew transliteration: Tsaddiq
Meaning: "Righteous," "Just"
2 Chronicles 12:6; Ezra 9:15; Nehemiah 9:8; etc.

865. Hebrew transliteration: Tsemach
Meaning: "Bud," "Branch," "Sprout," "Shoot" of David from David's family tree
refers to the Messiah
Jeremiah 23:5; 33:15; Isaiah 4:2; Zec. 3:8; 6:12

866. Hebrew transliteration: Tsemach Adonai
Meaning: "Branch of the Lord"
Isaiah 4:2; Jeremiah 23:5; 33:15; Hosea 8:7; Zechariah 3:8; 6:12

867. Hebrew transliteration: Tsur
Meaning "Rock," "Strength"
Psalm 18:2

868. Hebrew transliteration: Tsur Yisrael
Meaning: "Rock of Israel"
2 Samuel 23:3

869. Hebrew transliteration: Tsur Yeshuato
Meaning: "Rock of His Salvation"
Deuteronomy 32:15

870. The Vine
refers to Jesus Christ
John 15:5

871. Who will have all men to be saved
1 Timothy 2:4

872. Who also maketh intercession for us
refers to Jesus Christ
Romans 8:34 KJV
NASB: "Who…intercedes for us"

ESB: "Who indeed is interceding for us"

873. Who answered me in the day of my distress
Genesis 35:3 KJV

874. Who calleth those things which be not as though they were
Romans 4:17 KJV
NASB: "Who… calls into being that which does not exist"

875. Who comforteth us in all our tribulation
2 Corinthians 1:4 KJV
NKJV: "Who comforts us in all our tribulation"
NASB, ESV: "Who comforts us in all our affliction"

876. Who commanded the light to shine out of darkness
2 Corinthians 4:6 KJV

877. Who coverest thyself with light as with a garment
Psalm 104:2 KJV
NKJV: "Who cover Yourself with light as with a garment"
NASB: "Covering Yourself with light as with a cloak"

878. Who crowneth thee with loving-kindness and tender mercies
Psalm 103:4; Psalm 119:156; Psalm 145:9 KJV
NASB: "Who crowns you with lovingkindness and tender mercies"

879. Who daily bears our burden
Psalm 68:19 NASB

880. Who dwelleth on high
Psalm 113:5 KJV
NKJV: "Who dwells on high" NASB: "Who is enthroned on high"
ESV: "Who is seated on high"
881. Who forgiveth all thine iniquities
Psalm 103:3 KJV
882. Who gave himself a ransom for all
refers to Jesus Christ
1 Timothy 2:6 KJV
NKJV, NASB, ESV: "Who gave Himself as a ransom for all"
883. Who gave himself for our sins
refers to Jesus Christ
Galatians 1:4
884. Who giveth food to all flesh
Psalm 136:25 KJV
885. Who giveth rain upon the Earth
Job 5:10 KJV
886. Who giveth songs in the night
Job 35:10 KJV
887. Who giveth us richly all things to enjoy
1 Timothy 6:17 KJV
888. Who hath abolished death
2 Timothy 1:10 KJV
refers to Jesus Christ
889. Who hath also sealed us
2 Corinthians 1:22 KJV
refers to Jesus Christ
890. Who hath ascended up into heaven
Proverbs 30:4 KJV
891. Who hath bound the waters in a gar-

ment
Proverbs 30:4 KJV

892. Who hath called us unto his eternal glory by Christ Jesus
1 Peter 5:10 KJV

893. Who hath called you unto his kingdom and glory
1 Thessalonians 2:12 KJV

894. Who hath established all the ends of the Earth
Proverbs 30:4 KJV

895. Who hath gathered the wind in His fists
Proverbs 30:4 KJV

896. Who hath given me counsel
Psalm 16:7 KJV

897. Who hath given the earnest of the Spirit in our hearts
refers to Jesus Christ
2 Corinthians 1:22 KJV

898. Who hath his eyes like unto a flame of fire
refers to Jesus Christ
Revelation 2:18 KJV

899. Who hath redeemed my soul out of all adversity
2 Samuel 4:9 KJV

900. Who hath redeemed us from our enemies
Psalm 136:24 KJV

901. Who hath saved us and called us with a holy calling
2 Timothy 1:9 KJV

902. Who hast done great things
Psalm 71:19 KJV
903. Who hast set thy glory above the heavens
Psalm 8:1 KJV
904. Who healeth all thy diseases
Psalm 103:3 KJV
905. Who humbleth himself to behold the things that are in heaven and in the Earth
906. Who is above all, and through all
Ephesians 4:6 KJV
907. Who is blessed for ever
Romans 1:25; 9:5 KJV
908. Who is over all
refers to Jesus Christ
Romans 9:5 KJV
909. Who is rich in mercy
Ephesians 2:4 KJV
910. Who is worthy to be praised
2 Samuel 22:4; Psalm 18:3 KJV
911. Who keepest covenant and mercy
1 Kings 8:23; Nehemiah 9:32 KJV
912. Who laid the foundations of the Earth, that it should not be removed for ever
Psalm 104:5 KJV
913. Who layeth the beams of his chambers in the waters
Psalm 104:3 KJV
914. Who liveth for ever and ever
Daniel 4:34; Revelation 4:9; 10:6; 15:7 KJV
915. Who loved me, and gave himself for me
refers to Jesus Christ

Galatians 2:20 KJV

916. Who maketh the clouds his chariot
Psalm 104:3 KJV

917. Who maketh his angels spirits; his ministers a flaming fire
Psalm 104:4; Hebrews 1:7 KJV

918. Who only doeth wondrous things
Psalm 72:18 KJV

919. Who only hath immortality
1 Timothy 6:16 KJV

920. Who quickeneth all things
1 Timothy 6:13 KJV

921. Who quickeneth the dead
John 5:21; Romans 4:17 KJV

922. Who redeemeth thy life from destruction
Psalm 103:4 KJV

923. Who remembered us in our low estate
Psalm 136:23 KJV

924. Who satisfieth thy mouth with good things
Psalm 103:5 KJV

925. Who shall establish you, and keep you from evil
2 Thessalonians 3:3

926. Who stretchest out the heavens like a curtain
Psalm 104:2 KJV

927. Who taketh vengeance
Romans 3:5 KJV

928. Who walketh upon the wings of the wind

Psalm 104:3 KJV

929. Who was delivered for our offenses
Romans 4:25 KJV
refers to Jesus Christ

930. Who was faithful to him that appointed him
refers to Jesus Christ
Hebrews 3:2 KJV

931. Who was raised again for our justification
refers to Jesus Christ
Romans 4:25 KJV

932. Who was with me in the way which I went
Genesis 35:3 KJV

933. The Word
refers to Jesus Christ
John 1:1

934. The Word of God
refers to Jesus Christ
Revelation 19:13

935. Wonderful Hebrew transliteration: peleh or pele'
Isaiah 9:6

936. Hebrew transliteration: Yah—consists of the first two letters of YHWH (below)

937. Hebrew transliteration: Yahweh or YHWH or YHVH
Pious Jews carefully avoid saying this name, and substitute such words as Hashem, Adonai, "The Name," etc.

938. Hebrew transliteration: Yahweh Elohe

Tsebaoth
    Amos 4:13 NOG
    939. Hebrew transliteration: Yashar
    Meaning: "Just One"
    Isaiah 26:7
    940. Greek transliteration: Yeos

    Meaning: "God"
    941. Hebrew transliteration: Yesua or Yesha
    See: Jesus and Joshua
    942. Your dread
    943. Your fear
    944. Your heavenly Father
    Matthew 6:14; 6:26, 32; Luke 11:13
    945. Your Holy One
    Isaiah 43:15
    946. Your King
    Isaiah 43:15
    947. Hebrew transliteration: Yĕhowshuwa or Y'shua or d or Joshua or Jesus
    Meaning: "Jehovah is Salvation"
    948. Hebrew transliteration: Zebaot
    949. Hebrew transliteration: Zur or Tsur
    Meaning: Rock

FOUR

# Names, Titles, Descriptions, Truths & Characters of Jesus Christ, the Lord God Almighty

I.—And Simon Peter answered and said, 'You are the Christ, the Son of the Living God.' Mat 16:16

The Son  1 Jo 4:14
The Son of God Jhn 1:34
The Son of the living God Mat 16:16
His only begotten Son Jhn 3:16
The Son of the Father 1Jo 1:3
The only begotten of the Father Jhn 1:14
The only begotten Son, which is in the bosom of the Father Jhn 1:18
The first-born of every creature Col 1:15
His own Son Rom 8:32
A Son given Isa 9:6
One Son (his well-beloved) Mar 12:6
My Son Psa 2:7

His dear Son (or the Son of his love) Col 1:13
The Son of the Highest Luk 1:32
The Son of the Blessed Mar 14:61
Secret Jdg 13:18
Wonderful Isa 9:6

Testimony borne to the Son by the Father, by Jesus Himself, by the Spirit, by Angels, saints, men and devils.

The Father, "My Beloved Son." Mat 17:5
Jesus Himself, "I am the Son of God." Jhn 10:36
The Spirit, "The Son of God." Mar 1:1
Gabriel, "The Son of God." Luk 1:35; 2:11
John Baptist, "This is the Son of God." Jhn 1:34
John, Apostle, "The Christ, the Son of God." Jhn 20:31
Paul, Apostle, "He is the Son of God." Act 9:20
Disciples, "You are the Son of God." Mat 14:33
Nathaniel, "Rabbi, you are the Son of God." Jhn 1:49
Martha, "The Christ, the Son of God." Jhn 11:27
Eunuch, "Jesus Christ is the Son of God." Act 8:37
Centurion, "Truly this was the Son of God." Mar 15:39
Unclean spirits, "You are the Son of God." Mar 3:11

The Legion, "You Son of the Most High God." Mar 5:7

II.—But to the Son He says: "Your throne, O God, is forever and ever." Hbr 1:8
God Jhn 1:1; Mat 1:23; Isa 40:3
Thy throne, O God, is for ever and ever Hbr 1:8
The Mighty God Isa 9:6
The Everlasting God Isa 40:28
The True God 1Jo 5:20
My Lord and my God Jhn 20:28
God my Saviour Luk 1:47
Over all, God blessed for ever. Amen Rom 9:5
The God of the whole earth Isa 54:5
God manifest in the flesh 1Ti 3:16
Our God and Savior 2Pe 1:1
The great God and our Saviour, Jesus Christ Tts 2:13
Emanuel, God with us Mat 1:23
The God of Abraham, The God of Isaac, The God of Jacob Exd 3:2, 6
The Highest Luk 1:76

III.—Truly, truly, I say to you, Before Abraham was, I am. Jhn 8:58. Holy, Holy, Holy is the Lord of Hosts. Isa 6:3
Jehovah Isa 40:3
The Lord Jehovah Isa 40:10
Jehovah my God Zec 14:5
Jehovah of Hosts Isa 6:3; Jhn 12:41

Jehovah, God of Hosts Hsa 12:4, 5; Gen 32:24
The King, Jehovah of Hosts Isa 6:5
The Strong and Mighty Jehovah Psa 24:8
Jehovah, mighty in battle Psa 24:8
The Man, Jehovah's Fellow Zec 13:7
Jehovah-tsidkenu (the Lord our righteousness) Jer 23:6
The Lord Rom 10:13; Joe 2:32
The Lord of Glory 1Cr 2:8
The Same Hbr 1:12; Psa 102:27
I am Exd 3:14; Jhn 8:24
I am (before Abraham was) Jhn 8:58
I am (whom they sought to kill) Jhn 18:5, 6
I am (the Son of Man lifted up) Jhn 8:28
I am (the Resurrection and the Life) Jhn 11:25

IV.—He is before All things, and by Him all things consist. Col 1:17
The Almighty, which is, and which was, and which is to come Rev 1:8
The Creator of all things Col 1:16
The Upholder of all things Hbr 1:3
The Everlasting Father (or Father of Eternity) Isa 9:6
The Beginning Col 1:18
The Beginning and the Ending Rev 1:8
The Alpha and the Omega Rev 1:8
The First and the Last Rev 1:17
The Life 1Jo 1:2
Eternal Life 1Jo 5:20
That Eternal Life which was with the Father 1Jo 1:2

He that liveth Rev 1:18

V.—No one has seen God at any time. The only begotten Son, who is in the bosom of the Father, He has declared Him. . Jhn 1:18
The Word Jhn 1:1
The Word was with God Jhn 1:1
The Word was God Jhn 1:1
The Word of God Rev 19:13
The Word of Life 1Jo 1:1
The Word was made flesh Jhn 1:14
The Image of God 2Cr 4:4
The Image of the Invisible God Col 1:15
The Express Image of his Person Hbr 1:3
The Brightness of his Glory Hbr 1:3
Wisdom Pro 8:12, 22
The Wisdom of God 1Cr 1:24
The Power of God 1Cr 1:24
My Messenger Isa 42:19
The Messenger of the Covenant Mal 3:1
The Angel of Jehovah Gen 22:15
The Angel of God Gen 31:11, 13; Exd 14:19
The Angel of his presence Isa 63:9

VI.—You have made Him a little lower than the angels. Hbr 2:7
The Man Jhn 19:5
The Man Christ Jesus 1Ti 2:5
A Man approved of God Act 2:22
The Second Man, the Lord from heaven 1Cr 15:47
The Son of Man Mar 10:33

The Son of Abraham Mat 1:1
The Son of David Mat 1:1
The Son of Mary Mar 6:3
The Son of Joseph (reputed) Jhn 1:45
The Seed of the Woman Gen 3:15
The Seed of Abraham Gal 3:16, 19
Of the Seed of David Rom 1:3

VII.—Behold, I have come to do your will, O God. Hbr 10:9
The Babe Luk 2:12
The Child Isa 7:16
The Young Child Mat 2:20
A Child Born Isa 9:6
The Child Jesus Luk 2:43
Her First-Born Son Luk 2:7
The Sent of the Father Jhn 10:36
The Apostle Hbr 3:1
A Prophet Act 3:22, 23
A Great Prophet Luk 7:16
The Prophet of Nazareth Mat 21:11
A Prophet mighty in deed and word Luk 24:19
A Servant Phl 2:7
The Servant of the Father Mat 12:18
My Servant, O Israel Isa 49:3
My Servant, the Branch Zec 3:8
My Righteous Servant Isa 53:11
A Servant of Rulers Isa 49:7
A Nazarene, or Nazarite Mat 2:23
The Carpenter Mar 6:3
The Carpenter's Son (reputed) Mat 13:55

He Humbled Himself unto death Phl 2:8
A Stranger and an Alien Psa 69:8
A Man of Sorrows Isa 53:3
A Worm, and no Man Psa 22:6
Accursed of God (or the Curse of God) Deu 21:23

VIII.—God has given Him a name which is above every name. Phl 2:9, 10
Jesus Mat 1:21
Jesus Himself Luk 24:15
I, Jesus Rev 22:16
A Saviour, Jesus Act 13:23
The Saviour of the World 1Jo 4:14
A Saviour, which is Christ the Lord Luk 2:11
Jesus Christ Rev 1:5
The Lord Jesus Christ Col 1:2
Our Lord Jesus Christ Himself 2Th 2:16
Jesus the Christ Mat 16:20
Jesus Christ our Lord Rom 5:21
Jesus Christ the Righteous 1Jo 2:1
Jesus Christ, the same yesterday, to-day and for ever Hbr 13:8
Jesus of Nazareth Act 22:8
Jesus Christ of Nazareth Act 4:10
Lord Jesus Act 7:59
Christ Jesus 1Ti 1:15
Christ Mat 23:8
Messiah, which is called Christ Jhn 4:25
Anointed Psa 2:2; Act 4:27
Christ the Lord Luk 2:11
The Lord Christ Col 3:24

The Christ of God Luk 9:20
The Lord's Christ Luk 2:26
The Christ, the Son of the Blessed Mar 14:61
The Christ, the Saviour of the World Jhn 4:42

IX.—Worthy is the Lamb who was slain to receive power, riches, wisdom, strength, honor, glory and blessing. Rev 5:12
The Lamb of God Jhn 1:29
A Lamb without blemish and without spot 1Pe 1:19
The Lamb that was slain Rev 5:12
A Lamb as it had been slain Rev 5:6
The Lamb in the midst of the throne Rev 7:17
The Bridegroom Mat 9:15; Rev 21:9
The Lamb (the Temple of the City) Rev 21:22
The Lamb (the Light of the City) Rev 21:23
The Lamb (the Overcomer) Rev 17:14

X.—I will set up One Shepherd over them, and he will feed them. Eze 34:23
One Shepherd Jhn 10:16
Jehovah's Shepherd Zec 13:7
The Shepherd of the Sheep Hbr 13:20
The Way Jhn 14:6
The Door of the Sheep Jhn 10:7
The Shepherd of Israel Eze 34:23
The Shepherd and Bishop of Souls 1Pe 2:25
The Good Shepherd (that laid down his life) Jhn 10:11
The Great Shepherd (that was brought again from the dead) Hbr 13:20

The Chief Shepherd (that shall again appear) 1Pe 5:4

XI.—The Tree of Life in the midst of the Paradise of God. Rev 2:7
The Root of Jesse Isa 11:10
The Root of David Rev 5:5
The Root and Offspring of David Rev 22:16
A Rod out of the stem of Jesse Isa 11:1
A Branch out of his roots Isa 11:1
The Branch Zec 6:12
The Branch of the Lord Isa 4:2
The Branch of Righteousness Jer 33:15
A Righteous Branch Jer 23:5
The Branch strong for thyself Psa 80:15
The Vine Jhn 15:5
The True Vine Jhn 15:1
The Tree of Life Rev 2:7
The Corn of Wheat Jhn 12:24
The Bread of God Jhn 6:33
The True Bread from Heaven Jhn 6:32
The Bread which came down from Heaven Jhn 6:41
The Bread which cometh down from Heaven Jhn 6:50
The Bread of Life Jhn 6:35
The Living Bread Jhn 6:51
The Hidden Manna Rev 2:17
A Plant of Renown Eze 34:29
The Rose of Sharon Sgs 2:1
The Lily of the Valley Sgs 2:1
A Bundle of Myrrh Sgs 1:13

A Cluster of Camphire Sgs 1:14

XII.— I am the Light of the world; he who follows me shall posses the Light of life. Jhn 8:12
The Light Jhn 12:35
The True Light Jhn 1:9
A Great Light Isa 9:2
A Light came into the world Jhn 12:46
The Light of the world Jhn 8:12
The Light of men Jhn 1:4
A Light to lighten the Gentiles Luk 2:32
A Light of the Gentiles Isa 42:6
A Star Num 24:17
The Morning Star Rev 2:28
The Bright and Morning Star Rev 22:16
The Day Star 2Pe 1:19
The Day-spring from on High Luk 1:78
The Sun of Righteousness Mal 4:2

XIII.—The name of the Lord is a Strong Tower. Pro 18:10
The Strength of the children of Israel Joe 3:12-16
A Strength to the Poor Isa 25:4
A Strength to the needy in distress Isa 25:4
A Refuge from the Storm Isa 25:4
A Covert from the Tempest Isa 32:2
The Hope of his people Joe 3:12-16
A Horn of Salvation Luk 1:69

XIV.—They drank of that spiritual Rock that followed them, and that Rock was Christ. 1Cr

10:4
    The Rock Mat 16:18
    My Strong Rock Psa 31:2
    The Rock of Ages Isa 26:4
    The Rock that is higher than I Psa 61:2
    My Rock and my Fortress Psa 31:3
    The Rock of my Strength Psa 62:7
    The Rock of my Refuge Psa 94:22
    A Rock of Habitation Psa 71:3
    The Rock of my Heart Psa 73:26
    The Rock of my Salvation 2Sa 22:47
    My Rock and my Redeemer Psa 19:14
    That Spiritual Rock 1Cr 10:4
    The Rock that followed them 1Cr 10:4
    A Shadow from the Heat Isa 25:4

XV.—For no other foundation can anyone lay than that which is laid, which is Jesus Christ. 1Cr 3:11
    The Builder Hbr 3:3; Mat 16:18
    The Foundation 1Cr 3:11
    A Sure Foundation Isa 28:16
    A Stone Isa 28:16
    A Living Stone 1Pe 2:4
    A Tried Stone Isa 28:16
    A Chief Corner-stone 1Pe 2:6
    An Elect Stone 1Pe 2:6
    A Precious Stone 1Pe 2:6
    The Head Stone of the Corner Psa 118:22
    A Stone cut out without hands Dan 2:34, 45
    But unto them which are disobedient, –
    A Stone of Stumbling 1Pe 2:8

A Rock of Offense 1Pe 2:8

XVI.—And in His temple everyone says, "Glory!". Psa 29:9
The Temple Rev 21:22
A Sanctuary Isa 8:14
The Minister of the Sanctuary and of the True Tabernacle Hbr 8:2
Minister of the Circumcision Rom 15:8
The Veil (his flesh) Hbr 10:20
The Altar Hbr 13:10
The Offerer Hbr 7:27
The Offering Eph 5:2
The Sacrifice Eph 5:2
A Ransom (his life) Mar 10:49
The Lamb Rev 7:9
The Lamb Slain Rev 13:8
Within the Veil- –
The Forerunner (for us entered, even Jesus) Hbr 6:20
The Mercy-seat (or Propitiation) Rom 3:25
The Priest Hbr 5:6
The High Priest Hbr 3:1
The Great High Priest Hbr 4:14
The Mediator 1Ti 2:5
The Daysman Job 9:33
The Interpreter Job 33:23
The Intercessor Hbr 7:25
The Advocate 1Jo 2:1
The Surety Hbr 7:22

XVII.—A present is a precious stone in the

eyes of its possessor;
    Wherever he turns, he prospers. . Pro 17:8
    The Gift of God Jhn 4:10; 3:16
    His Unspeakable Gift 2Cr 9:15
    My Beloved, in whom my soul is well pleased Mat 12:18
    Mine Elect, in whom my soul delighteth Isa 42:1
    The Holy Child Jesus Act 4:27
    The Chosen of God Luk 23:35
    The Salvation of God Luk 2:30
    The Salvation of the daughter of Zion Isa 62:11
    The Redeemer Isa 59:20
    The Shiloh (Peace-Maker) Gen 49:10
    The Consolation of Israel Luk 2:25
    The Blessed Psa 77:17
    The Most Blessed for ever Psa 21:6

XVIII.—who was faithful to Him who appointed Him . Hbr 3:2
    The Truth Jhn 14:6
    The Faithful and True Rev 19:11
    A Covenant of the people Isa 42:6
    The Testator or Covenanter Hbr 9:16, 17
    The Faithful Witness Rev 1:5
    The Faithful and True Witness Rev 3:14
    A Witness to the People Isa 55:4
    The Amen Rev 3:14

XIX.—He that is Holy, he that is True. Rev 3:7

The Just 1Pe 3:18
The Just One Act 7:52
Thine Holy One Act 2:27
The Holy One and the Just Act 3:14
The Holy One of Israel Isa 49:7
The Holy One of God Mar 1:24
Holy, Holy, Holy Isa 6:3; Jhn 12:41

XX.—That in all things He might have the Pre-Eminence. Col 1:18

The Beginning of the Creation of God Rev 3:14
My First-Born Psa 89:27
The First-Born from the dead Col 1:18
The First-Begotten of the dead Rev 1:5
The First-Born among many Brethren Rom 8:29
The First-Fruits of them that slept 1Cr 15:20
The Last Adam 1Cr 15:45
The Resurrection Jhn 11:25
A Quickening Spirit 1Cr 15:45
The Head (even Christ) Eph 4:15
The Head of the Body, the Church Col 1:18
The Head over all things to the Church Eph 1:22
The Head of every Man 1Cr 11:3
The Head of all Principality and Power Col 2:10

XXI.—Gird your sword upon your thigh, O Mighty One, with your glory and your majesty. Psa 45:3

The Captain of the Host of the Lord Jos 5:14
The Captain of Salvation Hbr 2:10
The Author and Finisher of Faith Hbr 12:2
A Leader Isa 55:4
A Commander Isa 55:4
A Ruler Mic 5:2
A Governor Mat 2:6
The Deliverer Rom 11:26
The Lion of the Tribe of Judah Rev 5:5
An Ensign of the People Isa 11:10
The Chiefest among Ten Thousand (in an army) Sgs 5:10
A Polished Shaft Isa 49:2
The Shield Psa 84:9

XXII.—All Power in heaven and on earth is given to Me. Mat 28:18
The Lord 1Cr 12:3
One Lord Eph 4:5
God hath made that same Jesus both Lord and Christ Act 2:36
Lord of Lords Rev 17:14
King of Kings Rev 17:14
Lord both of the dead and living Rom 14:9
Lord of the Sabbath Luk 6:5
Lord of Peace 2Th 3:16
Lord of all Act 10:36
Lord over all Rom 10:12

XXIII.—Him God has exalted to His right hand to be Prince and Savior . Act 5:31
The Messiah the Prince Dan 9:25

The Prince of Life Act 3:15
A Prince and a Saviour Act 5:31
The Prince of Peace Isa 9:6
The Prince of Princes Dan 8:25
The Prince of the Kings of the earth Rev 1:5
A Prince (among Israel) Eze 34:24
The Glory of thy people Israel Luk 2:32
He who fills all in all Eph 1:23

XXIV.—He will reign for ever and ever. Rev 11:15

The Judge Act 17:31
The Righteous Judge 2Ti 4:8
The King Zec 14:16
The King of Kings Rev 19:16
Lord of Lords Rev 19:16
A Scepter (out of Israel) Num 24:17
The King's Son Psa 72:1
David their King Jer 30:9
The King of Israel Jhn 1:49
King of the daughter of Zion Jhn 12:15
The King of the Jews (born) Mat 2:2; 15:2
The King of the Jews (crucified) Jhn 19:19
The King of Saints or King of Nations Rev 15:3
King over all the Earth Zec 14:4, 5, 9
The King of Righteousness Hbr 7:2
The King of Peace Hbr 7:2
The King of Glory Psa 24:10
The King in his beauty Isa 33:17
He sits King for ever Psa 29:10
Crowned with a Crown of Thorns Jhn 19:2

Crowned with Glory and Honor Hbr 2:9

Crowned with a Crown of Pure Gold Psa 21:3

Crowned with many Crowns Rev 19:12

Allusions, Characteristics and Epithets

As a Refiner's Fire. As Fuller's Soap Mal 3:2

As the Light of the Morning when the sun riseth, a morning without clouds. As the Tender Grass by clear shining after rain 2Sa 23:4

As a Tender Plant (to God). As a Root out of a dry ground (to man) Isa 53:2

As Rain upon the mown grass. As Showers that water the earth Psa 72:6

As Rivers of Water in a dry place. As the Shadow of a great Rock in a weary land. As an Hiding-place from the wind Isa 32:2

As Ointment poured forth Sgs 1:3

Fairer than the Children of Men Psa 45:2

A glorious high Throne from the beginning is the place of our sanctuary Jer 17:12

For a Glorious Throne to his father's house Isa 22:23

A Crown of Glory and Beauty Isa 28:5

A Stone of Grace Pro 17:8

Nail fastened in a sure place Isa 22:23

A Brother born for adversity Pro 17:17

A Friend sticks closer than a brother Pro 18:24

A Friend loves at all times Pro 17:17

His Countenance is as the sun Rev 1:16

His Countenance is as Lebanon Sgs 5:15

Yea. He is altogether lovely. This is my be-

loved and my Friend Sgs 5:16
    Consider Him
    He was Obedient Phl 2:8
    He was Meek, Lowly Mat 11:29
    He was Guileless 1Pe 2:22
    He was Tempted Hbr 4:15
    He was Oppressed Isa 53:7
    He was Despised Isa 53:3
    He was Rejected Isa 53:3
    He was Betrayed Mat 27:3
    He was Condemned Mar 14:64
    He was Reviled 1Pe 2:23
    He was Scourged Jhn 19:1
    He was Mocked Mat 27:29
    He was Wounded Isa 53:5
    He was Bruised Isa 53:5
    He was Stricken Isa 53:4
    He was Smitten Isa 53:4
    He was Crucified Mat 27:35
    He was Forsaken Psa 22:1
    He is Merciful Hbr 2:17
    He is Faithful Hbr 2:17
    He is Holy, Harmless Hbr 7:26
    He is Undefiled Hbr 7:26
    He is Separate Hbr 7:26
    He is Perfect Hbr 5:9
    He is Glorious Isa 49:5
    He is Mighty Isa 63:1
    He is Justified 1Ti 3:16
    He is Exalted Act 2:33
    He is Risen Luk 24:6
    He is Glorified Act 3:13

The Lord is my Portion
My Maker, Husband Isa 54:5
My Well-beloved Sgs 1:13
My Saviour 2Pe 3:18
My Hope 1Ti 1:1
My Brother Mar 3:35
My Portion Jer 10:16
My Helper Hbr 13:6
My Physician Jer 8:22
My Healer Luk 9:11
My Refiner Mal 3:3
My Purifier Mal 3:3
My Lord, Master Jhn 13:13
My Servant Luk 12:37
My Example Jhn 13:15
My Teacher Jhn 3:2
My Shepherd Psa 23:1
My Keeper Jhn 17:12
My Feeder Eze 34:23
My Leader Isa 40:11
My Restorer Psa 23:3
My Resting-place Jer 50:6
My Meat (his flesh) Jhn 6:55
My Drink (his blood) Jhn 6:55
My Passover 1Cr 5:7
My Peace Eph 2:14
My Wisdom 1Cr 1:30
My Righteousness 1Cr 1:30
My Sanctification 1Cr 1:30
My Redemption 1Cr 1:30
My All in All Col 3:11

FIVE

# The Name "Jesus Christ"

The name "Jesus" in Hebrew literally means "God saves."

The English name "Jesus" comes from the Greek name "Iesous," which is a rendition of the Hebrew "Yeshua." The name is related to the Hebrew verb root "rescue" and one of its noun forms, yesua, "deliverance."

In the New Testament, which was written in Greek, Christ in the Greek is the word "christos," which means "anointed."

In the Old Testament, which was written in Hebrew, the word for "Messiah" is "mashiach," which also means "anointed." So, the Greek word for Christ, "christos," is the Greek equivalent for the Hebrew word for Messiah, "mashiach."

Therefore, His name could properly be written and spoken as, "Jesus the Anointed One."

And thou shalt
call his name Jesus,
Prince of Peace, Mighty God,
Wonderful Counselor, Holy One,
Lamb of God, Prince of Life,
Lord God Almighty,
Lion of the Tribe of Judah,
Root of David, Word of Life,
Author and Finisher of Our Faith,
Advocate, The Way, Dayspring,
Lord of All, I AM, Son of God,
Shepherd and Bishop of Souls,
Messiah, The Truth, Saviour,
Chief Cornerstone, King of Kings,
Righteous Judge, Light of the World,
Head of the Church, Morning Star,
Sun of Righteousness, Lord
Jesus Christ, Chief Shepherd,
Resurrection and Life,
Horn of Salvation, Governor,
The Alpha and Omega

# THE NAME JESUS CHRIST

Jesus – Matthew 1:21
Prince of Peace – Isaiah 9:6
Mighty God – Isaiah 9:6
Wonderful Counselor – Isaiah 9:6
Holy One – Mark 1:24
Lamb of God – John 1:29
Prince of Life – Acts 3:15
Lord God Almighty – Rev. 15:3
Lion of the Tribe of Judah – Rev. 5:5
Root of David – Rev. 22:16
Word of Life – 1 John 1:1
Author and Finisher of Our Faith – Heb. 12:2
Advocate – 1 John 2:1
The Way – John 14:6
Dayspring – Luke 1:78
Lord of All – Acts 10:36
I AM – John 8:58
Son of God – John 1:34
Shepherd and Bishop of Souls – 1 Pet. 2:25
Messiah – John 11:41
The Truth – John 14:6
Saviour – 2 Pet. 2:20
Chief Cornerstone – Eph. 2:20
King of Kings – Rev. 19:16
Righteous Judge – 2 Tim. 4:8
Light of the World – John 8:12
Head of the Church – Eph. 1:22
Morning Star – Rev. 22:16
Sun of Righteousness – Malachi 4:2
Lord Jesus Christ – Acts 15:11
Chief Shepherd – 1 Pet. 5:4
Resurrection and Life – John 11:2

Horn of Salvation – Luke 1:69
Governor – Matthew 2:6 – Micah 5:2
The Alpha and Omega – Revelation 1:8

You shall call
His name JESUS,
Immanuel, King, Ruler,
Lord, Son of God, Son of Man,
Teacher, the Christ, the Anointed,
Savior, Messiah, Lamb of God,
The Revelation of God,
Bread of Life, Light of the world,
I AM
The Door, The Good Shepherd,
The Resurrection and the Life,
The Way, Truth, and Life,
The Vine, Bright and Morning Star,
King of Kings and Lord of Lords,
The Alpha and Omega,
The Beginning and End,
The First and Last,
The Almighty,
The Amen

You shall call His name Jesus – Matthew 1:21
Son, Immanuel – Matthew 1:23 (angel of the Lord)
King – Matthew 2:2 (wise men)
Ruler – Matthew 2:6 – Micah 5:2
Lord – Matthew 3:3
Son of God – Matthew 3:17, Matthew 17:5
Son of Man – Matthew 11:19
Teacher – Matthew 23:10
The Christ – Matthew. 23:10
The Anointed – Matthew 23:10
Savior – Luke 3:20
Messiah – John 1:41
Lamb of God – John 1:29
The Revelation of God – John 1:1

John

The Bread of Life – John 6:35
The Living Bread – John 6:51
Light of the World – John 8:12
I AM – John 8:58
The Door of the Sheep – John 10:7
The Good Shepherd – John 10:11
The Resurrection and the Life – John 11:2
The Way, Truth, and Life – John 14:6
The Vine – John 15:5

Revelation

The Alpha and Omega, Beginning and End – Revelation 1:8
Almighty – Revelation 1:8
The First and the Last- Revelation 1:11
The Amen – Revelation 3:14

# Bibliography

Christian Answers, ChristianAnswers.net, http://www.christiananswers.net/dictionary/namesofgod.html

Blue Letter Bible, blueletterbible.org, https://www.blueletterbible.org/study/parallel/paral19.cfm

Bridge Books exists to exalt Jehovah God Almighty and His Son, the Lord Jesus Christ.

Made in United States
Orlando, FL
14 April 2025